**ES**

# CORELDRAW
## AN INTRODUCTION

# ABOUT THIS BOOK

*CorelDRAW: An Introduction* is an easy-to-follow overview of this large graphics program. It is for people who have experience creating graphics on a PC and who want to discover more.

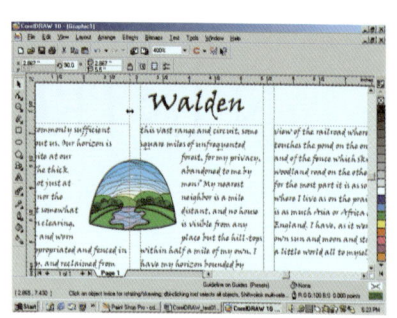

THE GRAPHICS SOFTWARE THAT IS bundled with Windows is adequate for many home-graphics projects. However, you may have design ideas that your present software cannot meet, and you may wonder what is offered by a professional graphics program. This book discusses a few of the numerous creative tools and options offered by one such software program, CorelDRAW 10. The book covers creative features, including line drawing tools, shape and text manipulation, and a multitude of different filling effects. You will also find out how to apply a number of 3-D effects to objects or text. Simple shapes and objects created early in the book are later altered and modified to help develop your knowledge and understanding of what this very powerful software package can do.

The chapters and the subsections present the information using step-by-step sequences. Virtually every step is accompanied by an illustration showing how your screen should look at each stage.

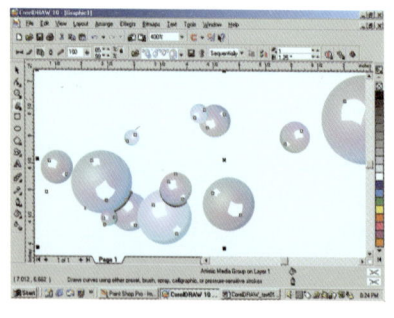

The book contains several features to help you understand both what is happening and what you need to do.

Command keys, such as ENTER and CTRL, are shown in these rectangles: Enter↵ and Ctrl, so that there's no confusion, for example, over whether you should press that key or type the letters "ctrl."

Cross-references are shown in the text as left- or right-hand page icons: ◁ and ▷. The page number and the reference are shown at the foot of the page.

As well as the step-by-step sections, there are boxes that explain a feature in detail, and tip boxes that provide alternative methods. Finally, at the back, you will find a glossary of common terms and a comprehensive index.

# ESSENTIAL DK COMPUTERS
# CORELDRAW
# AN INTRODUCTION

CHRIS DE LA NOUGEREDE

DK

## LONDON, NEW YORK, MUNICH, MELBOURNE, DELHI

Senior Editor Jacky Jackson
Senior Art Editor Sarah Cowley
US Editors Gary Werner and Margaret Parrish
DTP Designer Julian Dams
Production Controller Michelle Thomas

Managing Editor Adèle Hayward
Managing Art Editor Karen Self

Produced for Dorling Kindersley Limited by
Design Revolution Limited, Queens Park Villa,
30 West Drive, Brighton, England BN2 2GE
Editorial Director Ian Whitelaw
Senior Designer Andrew Easton
Project Editor John Watson
Designer Paul Bowler

First American Edition, 2002

01 02 03 04 05 10 9 8 7 6 5 4 3 2 1

Published in the United States by DK Publishing, Inc.,
95 Madison Avenue, New York, New York 10016

A Penguin Company

Copyright © 2002 Dorling Kindersley Limited
Text copyright © 2002 Dorling Kindersley Limited

All rights reserved under International and Pan-American Copyright Conventions. No part of this publication may be reproduced, stored in a retrieval system, or transmitted in any form or by any means, electronic, mechanical, photocopying, recording, or otherwise, without the prior written permission of the copyright owner. Published in Great Britain by Dorling Kindersley Limited.

DK Publishing offers special discounts for bulk purchases for sales promotions or premiums. Specific, large-quantity needs can be met with special editions, including personalized covers, excerpts of existing guides, and corporate imprints. For more information, contact Special Markets Department, DK Publishing, Inc., 95 Madison Avenue, New York, NY 10016 Fax: 800-600-9098.

A Cataloging-in-Publication record is available for this title from the Library of Congress.

ISBN 0-7894-8408-0

Color reproduced by Colourscan, Singapore
Printed and bound in Italy by Graphicom

See our complete catalog at
**www.dk.com**

# Contents

| 6 | **CorelDRAW Basics** |
| 12 | **Setting Up Your Page** |
| 22 | **Starting To Draw** |
| 36 | **Handling Objects** |
| 46 | **Working With Text** |
| 56 | **Fills And Colors** |
| 62 | **3-D Effects** |

Glossary 70 • Index 71 • Acknowledgments 72

# CorelDRAW Basics

CorelDRAW is one of the most comprehensive graphics packages available. Its user-friendly tools and intuitive controls make it a pleasure to use, even for people with little experience.

## What Can CorelDRAW Do?

Whether you want to produce basic drawings, complex illustrations, logos, greeting cards, catalogs, postage stamps, books, or billboards, CorelDRAW has all the versatility and power you need.

CorelDRAW has the flexibility to create a document up to 999 pages long. Each page can be a different size and CorelDRAW allows those pages to range from 0.1 inches to 150 feet in size.

### WHAT ELSE DOES CORELDRAW HAVE?

In addition to the graphics-handling capabilities that comprise the bulk of this book, CorelDRAW's word-processing and text-handling capabilities are second-to-none. It has numerous formatting and editing options, and virtually limitless creative potential in its effects.

CorelDRAW 10's versatile and comprehensive package also includes Corel PHOTO PAINT – an image editing program, and Corel R.A.V.E. – an animation program.

*There is a range of text formats in CorelDRAW for different purposes and for effects that are unavailable on any word processor.*

# Launching CorelDRAW

Despite its size and versatility, Corel-DRAW launches in exactly the same way as any other program running in Windows. It can be run alongside other software, and it is possible to exchange data between CorelDRAW and other applications.

## 1 LAUNCHING VIA THE START MENU

- From the Windows desktop, left-click on the **Start** button on the taskbar.
- Move the cursor up the pop-up menu until **Programs** is highlighted. A submenu appears.
- Choose **CorelDRAW 10** from the submenu, Another submenu appears containing CorelDRAW 10 applications.
- Click on the **CorelDRAW 10** option to launch the program.

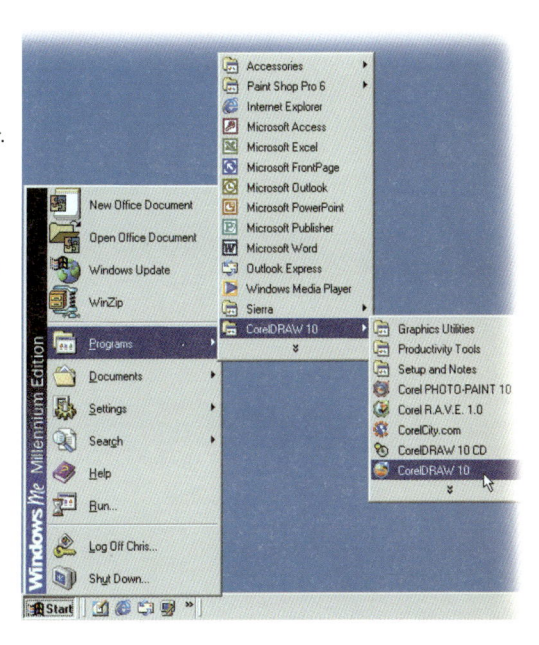

## 2 LAUNCHING VIA A SHORTCUT

- You may have a shortcut to CorelDRAW 10 on your desktop.
- If so, double-click on the shortcut to launch CorelDRAW 10.

# THE CORELDRAW WINDOW

The CorelDRAW window contains many features. It is the launchpad for pages of potentially very large images, as well as a storehouse of creative tools and a wide variety of stylistic options. The tools are out of sight, but they can be activated by clicking on their buttons. With the window in its initial state, it is not a case of "what you see is what you get" – there is much more waiting in the wings.

## WINDOW KEY

1. Title bar
2. Menu bar
3. Standard toolbar
   *This contains buttons for frequent actions.*
4. Property toolbar
   *This toolbar contains the main options for objects.*
5. Toolbox
   *Main tool options.*
6. Rulers
   *To determine size, space, and position.*
7. Drawing window
   *Storage for objects.*
8. Drawing page
   *Area for document.*
9. Scroll-up arrow
   *To move toward the top of the document.*
10. Vertical scroll bar
    *This contains the scroll button.*
11. Vertical scroll button
    *Moves page up or down.*
12. Scroll-down arrow
    *To move toward the end of the document.*

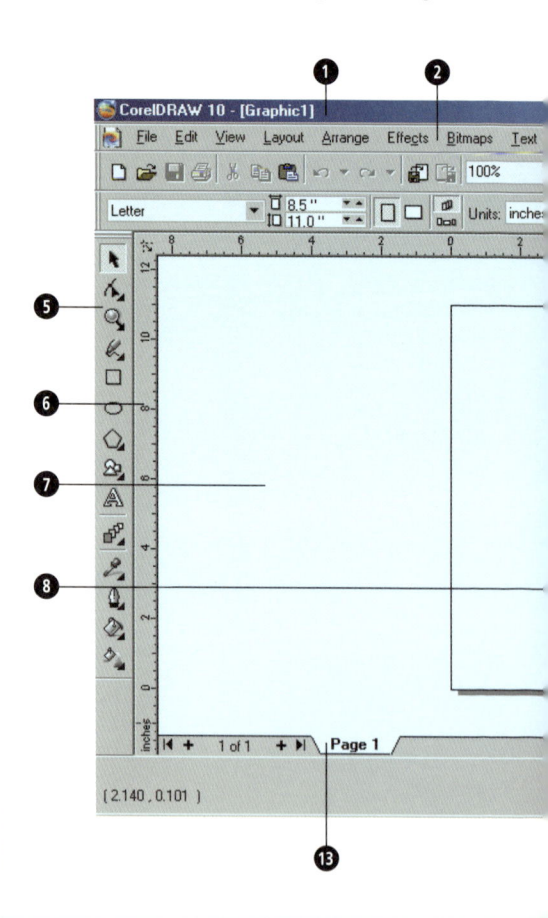

## THE CORELDRAW WINDOW • 9

### CORELDRAW'S INTERFACE

When setting out to design CorelDRAW 10, the makers set themselves the task of creating a user interface that was "intuitive, easier to navigate, and more efficient and customizable than its previous versions." The consensus is that they have been successful, particularly with improvements in the ability to access tools and change the properties of any object. Improved navigation means that CorelDRAW is now even easier to learn.

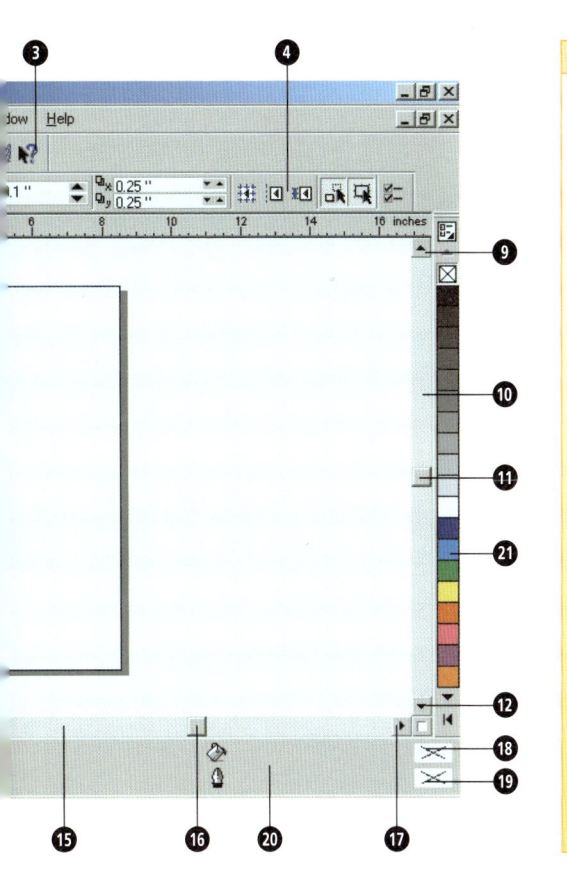

### WINDOW KEY

**13** Page tabs *These are used to navigate pages.*
**14** Left-scroll button *To move toward the left-hand side of the document.*
**15** Horizontal scroll bar *This contains the scroll button.*
**16** Horizontal scroll button *To move the page left or right.*
**17** Right-scroll button *To move toward the right-hand side of the document.*
**18** Fill display box *Details the kind of object fill.*
**19** Outline display box *Details the kind of object outline.*
**20** Status bar *Contains information regarding objects.*
**21** Default CMYK palette *Color options.*

# CorelDRAW Toolbars

The toolbars in CorelDRAW are not static. Depending on what is selected, whether it is an object, a piece of text, or even a guideline, a different property bar appears on-screen.

The tools, too, have their own property bars. Throughout the book, various flyout toolbars are referred to. Here, these flyout toolbars have been detached from the toolbox for clarity.

### TOOLBARS KEY

❶ Paper type and its associated size
❷ Portrait or landscape orientation
❸ Set default or current page size and orientation
❹ Snap to grid/guidelines/objects
❺ Pick tool
❻ Shape tool
❼ Zoom tool
❽ Freehand tool
❾ Bezier tool
❿ Artistic media tool
⓫ Dimension tool
⓬ Interactive connector tool
⓭ Rectangle tool
⓮ Ellipse tool
⓯ Polygon tool
⓰ Spiral tool
⓱ Graph paper tool
⓲ Basic shapes
⓳ Arrow shapes
⓴ Flowchart shapes
㉑ Star shapes

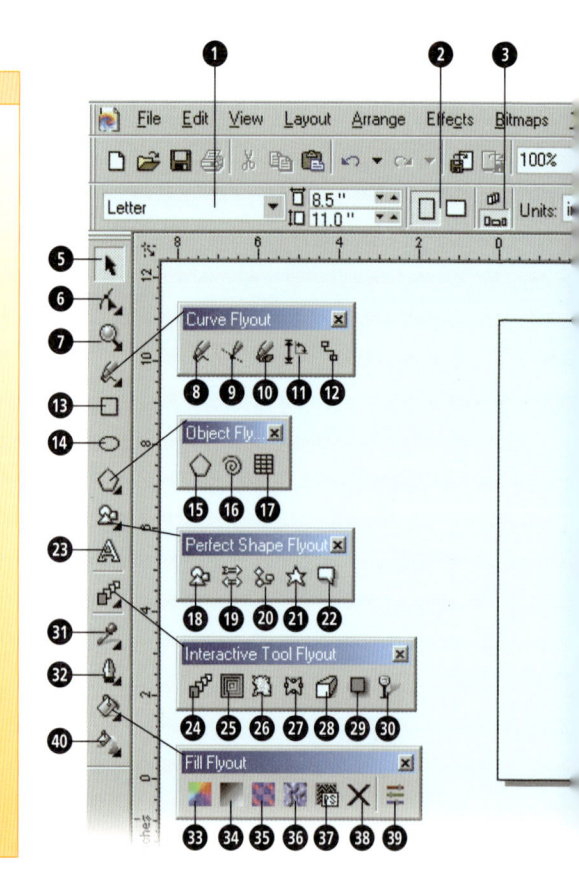

## CORELDRAW TOOLBARS · 11

### CUSTOMIZING TOOLBARS

It is possible to create new toolbars containing specific tools very easily, or move tool positions between existing toolbars. You can, for example, move a copy of the **Pick Tool** to the standard toolbar by holding down Ctrl and Alt, clicking on the **Pick Tool**, and dragging it between different locations. This flexibility means that you can easily move or copy tools, command buttons, options, and selectors between menus, toolbars, or the toolbox.

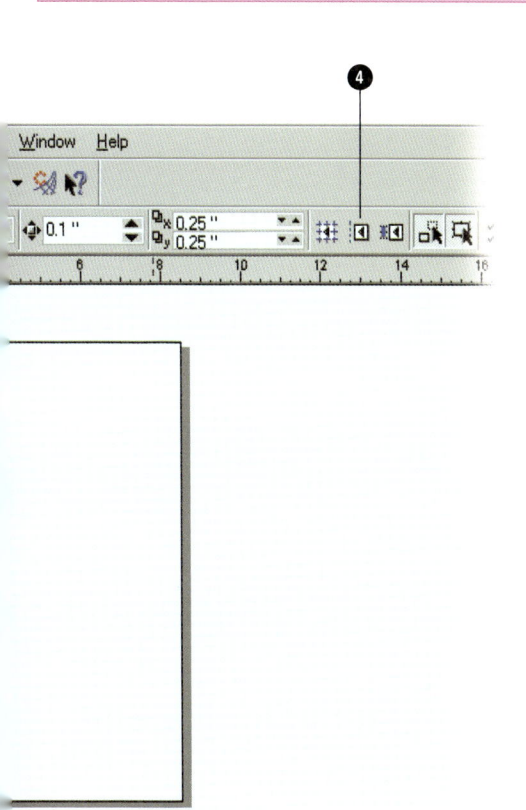

### TOOLBARS KEY

- ㉒ Callout shapes
- ㉓ Text tool
- ㉔ Interactive blend tool
- ㉕ Interactive contour tool
- ㉖ Interactive distortion tool
- ㉗ Interactive envelope tool
- ㉘ Interactive extrude tool
- ㉙ Interactive drop-shadow tool
- ㉚ Interactive transparency tool
- ㉛ Eyedropper tool
- ㉜ Outline tool
- ㉝ Fill color dialog
- ㉞ Fountain fill dialog
- ㉟ Pattern fill dialog
- ㊱ Texture fill dialog
- ㊲ PostScript fill dialog
- ㊳ No fill
- ㊴ Color docker window
- ㊵ Interactive fill tool

# Setting Up Your Page

The default page settings may suit your document, but you will probably want to make changes. Page size, orientation, and the number and order of pages can all be set as required.

## Opening the Drawing Window

When you launch CorelDRAW for the first time, you will be shown a **Welcome to CorelDRAW** screen containing a number of options. You can prevent this window from opening when you start the program by clicking in the check box at bottom left.

### THE WELCOME SCREEN OPTIONS
- **New Graphic** Click on this option to open a new document.
- **Open Last Edited** To resume work on the last document you worked on.
- **Open Graphic** To launch the browser in order to open an existing document.
- **Template** Opens an options menu containing various templates to use.
- **CorelTUTOR** Opens a step-by-step guide to several instructive projects with an option for online tutorials.
- **What's New?** Opens a menu of information about the new features contained in CorelDRAW 10.

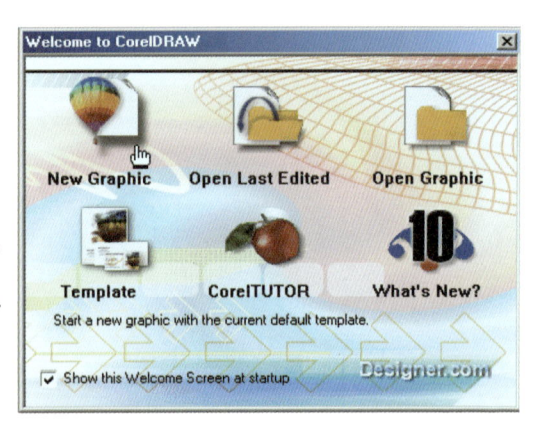

### THE DRAWING WINDOW

The drawing window is the whole area around the document page, and the page itself. You can use the space around the page like a table top to store objects that you may want to use in the document.

# Selecting the Page Details

CorelDRAW is a page-based application. You can choose the size of your pages from a list of preset dimensions, or create a custom-sized page. Decide on the page orientation – landscape or portrait – with the click of a button.

## 1 SELECTING YOUR PAGE SIZE
- To choose from one of 54 preset dimensions for your page size, click on the **Paper Type/Size** drop-down arrow and scroll to find the appropriate type.

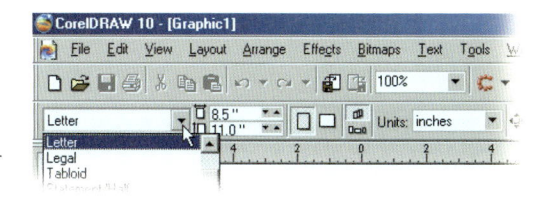

## 2 CREATING A CUSTOM SIZE
- The width and height of customized pages can be selected by using the **Paper Width and Height** scroll buttons.

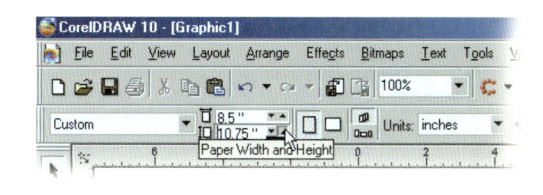

## 3 LANDSCAPE OR PORTRAIT
- Choose your page orientation by clicking on the **Landscape** or **Portrait** icon on the property bar.

*A preset size*
If your customized page corresponds with a preset size, its name appears in the **Paper Type/Size** box.

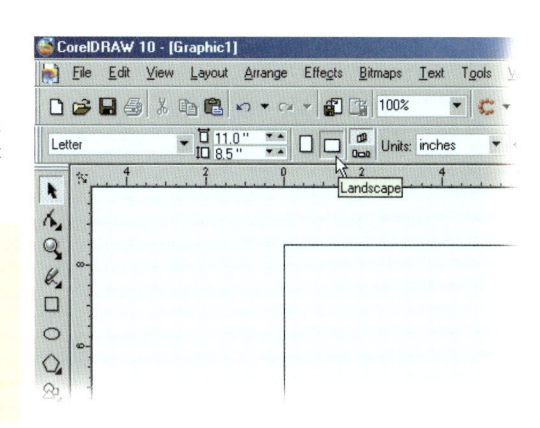

# INSERTING AND DELETING PAGES

You can add as many pages as you want to your document very easily. However, CorelDRAW has a maximum number of pages that it will allow in any one document, and this maximum is 999 pages. Deleting pages is equally easy.

## 1 INSERTING PAGES

- Click on **Layout** in the menu bar and choose **Insert Page** from the drop-down menu.

- In the **Insert Page** dialog box, use the scroll buttons to select the number of pages to be inserted.

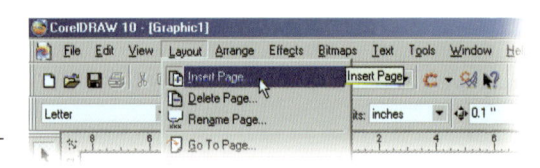

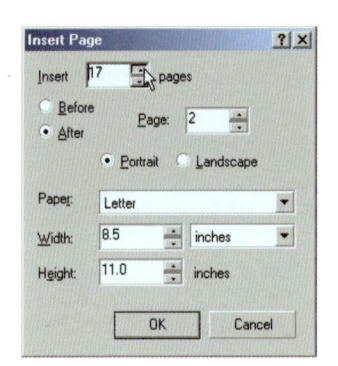

- Click on **OK** when you have entered the required number of pages.

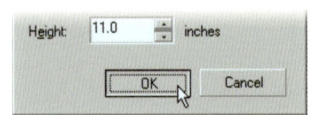

## 2 DELETING PAGES

- To delete pages, click on **Layout** in the menu bar and choose **Delete Page**.

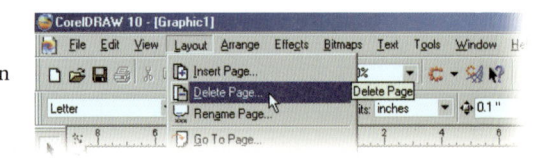

# HANDLING MULTI-PAGE DOCUMENTS · 15

- In the **Delete Page** dialog box, either type in or use the scroll buttons to select the first page number in the sequence that you want to delete.

- Check the **Through to page** box to select the final page number in the sequence you want to delete.

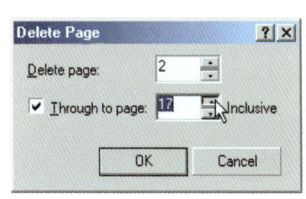

- When the correct range has been selected, click on **OK**.

# HANDLING MULTIPAGE DOCUMENTS

In a multipage document, you will sometimes want to see how the pages flow visually. **Page Sorter View** ia new to CorelDRAW 10, and in this mode, you can look at the pages as thumbnails (miniature versions in a low resolution).

## 1 MAKING PAGE SIZES IDENTICAL

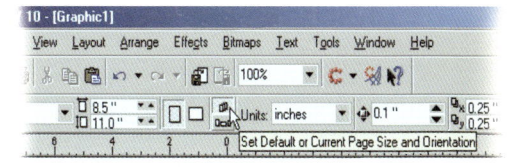

- In certain documents, such as a catalog or booklet, all the pages need to be set to an identical size throughout.
- To achieve this, click on the top **Set Default or Current Page Size and Orientation** icon on the property bar. This button ensures that when the size of one page is changed, all the other pages in the document are also changed at the same time.

# 16 · SETTING UP YOUR PAGE

- For documents that are to contain pages of different sizes, click on the bottom **Set Default or Current Page Size and Orientation**. You can now insert pages of whatever size you require.

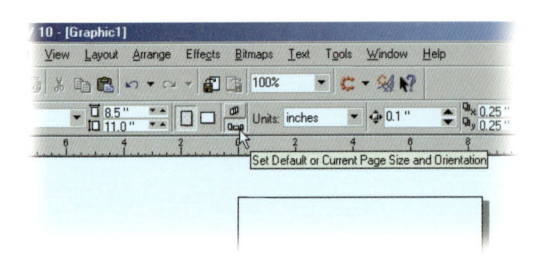

## 2 VIEWING A MULTI-PAGE DOCUMENT

- After you have experimented with inserting pages of different sizes, you can view the pages that you have created in your document as thumbnails.
- Click on **View** in the menu bar and select **Page Sorter View**.

- The pages that make up this document are of different sizes. However, the **Page Sorter View** does not show them in proportion. The business card, **Page 2**, looks almost as large as the letterhead, **Page 1**.

- To return to your document, click on the **Page Sorter View** icon in the property bar.

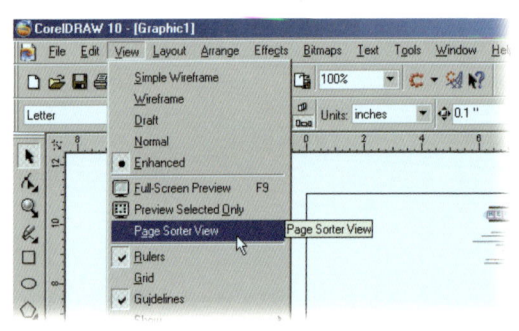

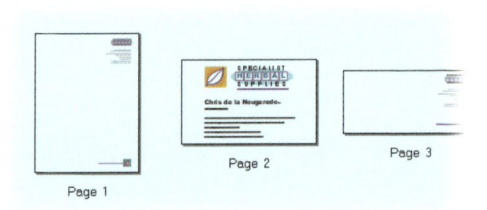

## 3 CHANGING THE PAGE ORDER

- The tabs at the bottom of each page can be clicked on and dragged to a new position in the document.

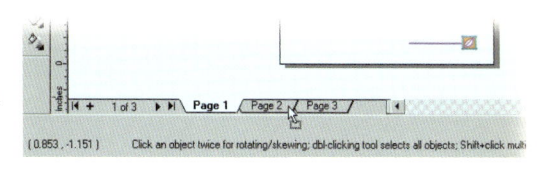

- You can also change the order of your pages in the **Page Sorter View** by clicking on one of the thumbnails and dragging it to the new position. Here **Page 2** has been selected and is being dragged to the position of **Page 1**.

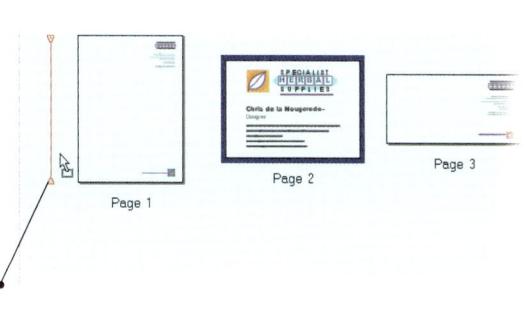

*Page 2 being dragged to precede Page 1*

# USING GUIDELINES

Guidelines can be inserted anywhere on your page, helping you to position and align objects precisely. They can be horizontal, vertical, or angled. A selected guideline is a different color from one that is not selected, and it is possible to change the color of guidelines. This is very useful if you need various sets of guidelines on the same document. CorelDRAW also has several preset guidelines available.

## 1 SETTING GUIDELINES

- Guidelines can be dragged from the side or top rulers.
- Here, the cursor has been clicked on the side ruler and dragged onto the page. Release the button when the line is correctly placed.

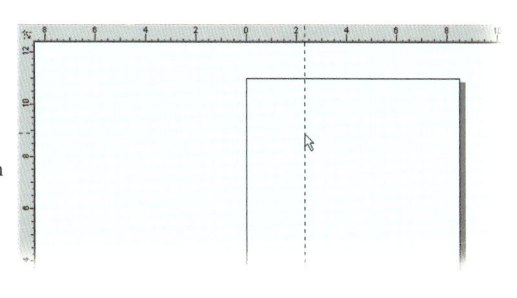

# 18 · SETTING UP YOUR PAGE

## 2 ROTATING GUIDELINES

- To create a guideline set at an angle, select it with the **Pick Tool** from the toolbox, and click on it again. A center of rotation appears, along with two skewing handles at the top and bottom of the guideline.

- Click on one of the skewing handles and hold down the left mouse button as you drag the guideline to its new angle of skew.

- When you release the mouse button and click the **Pick Tool** off the guideline, it assumes the new angle.

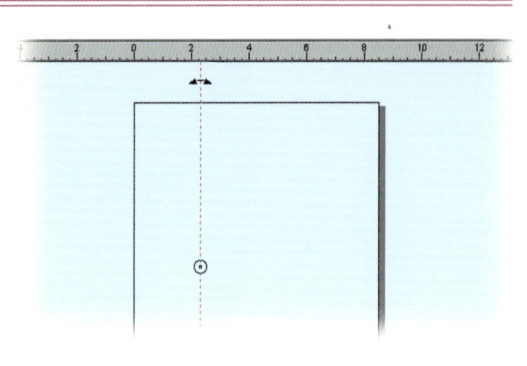

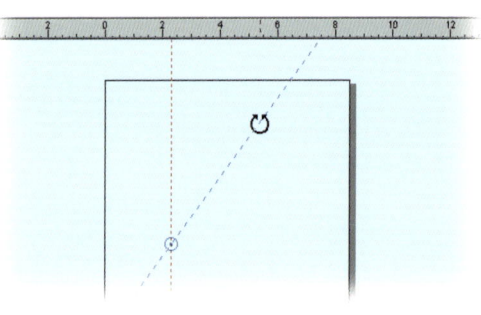

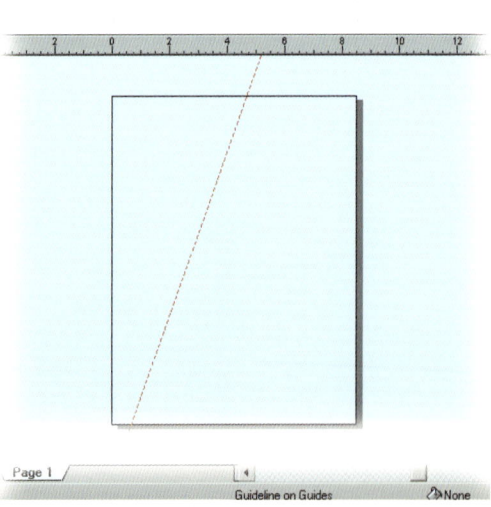

## USING GUIDELINES · 19

## 3 APPLYING PRESET GUIDELINES

- Click on **View** in the menu bar, and select **Guideline Setup**.

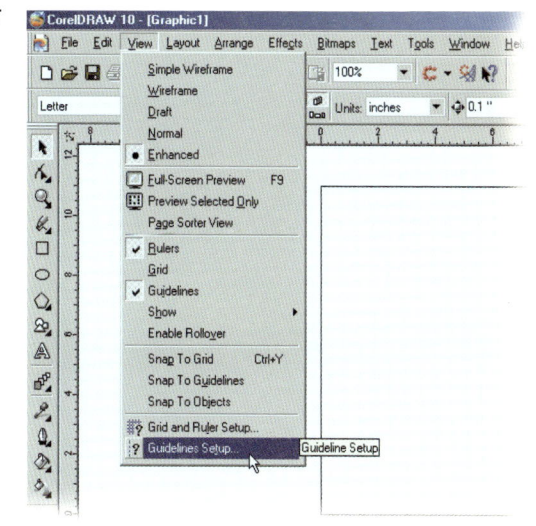

- The **Options** window opens.

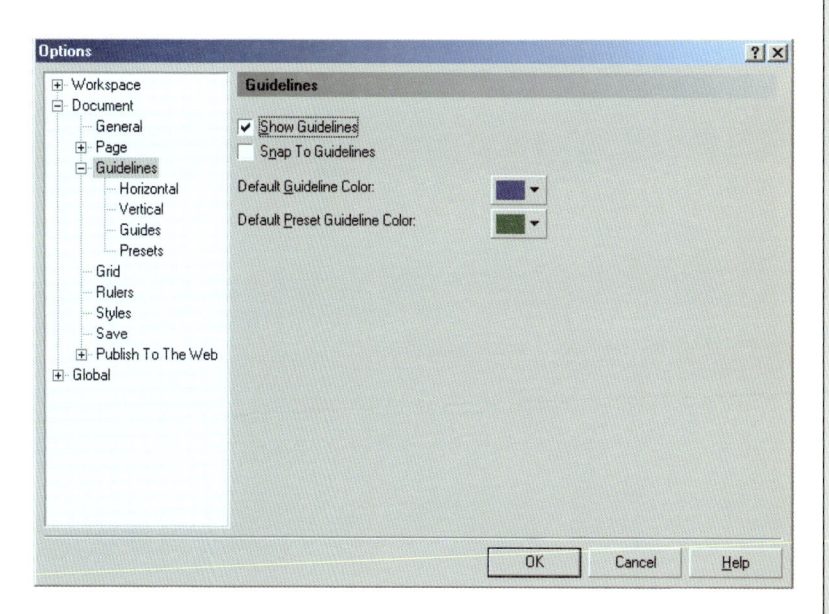

## 20 • SETTING UP YOUR PAGE

- From the options available, click on **Presets**.

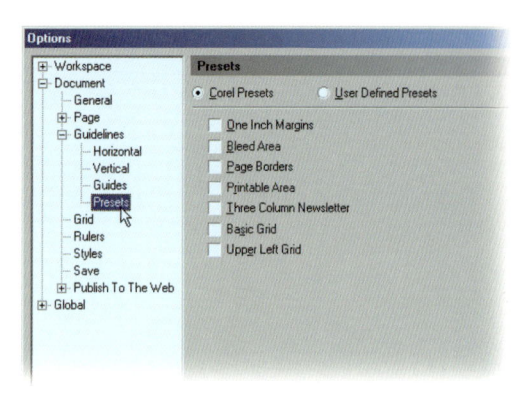

- From the range available, check the box of the preset that you want to apply to your page. Here, we have chosen the **Three Column Newsletter** option.
- Click the **Apply Presets** button to establish this as your selection.

- Click on **OK** to close the **Options** menu and to return to your page.

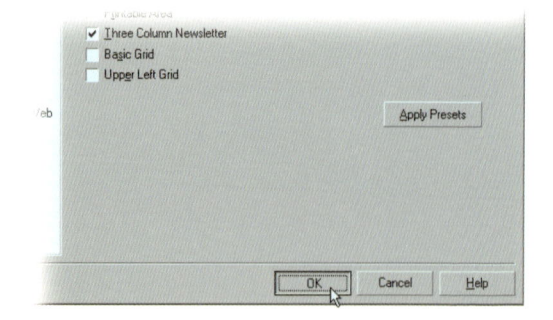

## USING GUIDELINES · 21

### 4 LOCKING GUIDELINES

- Once a guideline, or set of guidelines, has been satisfactorily positioned, it can be locked into place to prevent it from moving accidentally.
- To do this, click on the line or lines to select, then click on the **Lock** icon in the property bar.

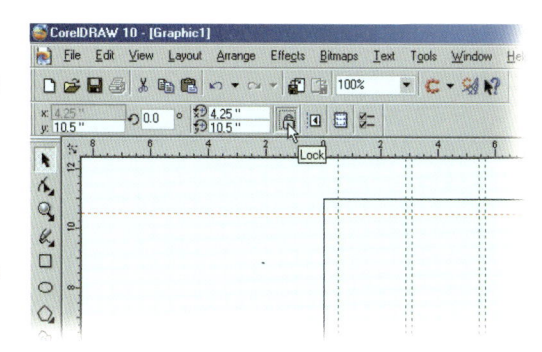

### 5 SNAPPING TO THE GUIDELINE

- Any object can be snapped into place next to a guideline.
- Select a guideline by clicking on it, then click on the **Snap To Guidelines** icon in the property bar.

- Any object that is now moved close to any guideline will snap to it. The most prominent tip(s) of the object will snap to the guideline, or the central point will snap into place if brought close to the guideline.

*Relevant part of the guideline to which the object is aligned*

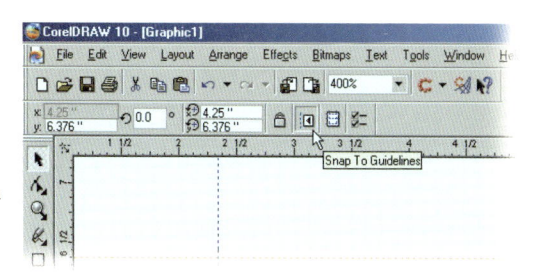

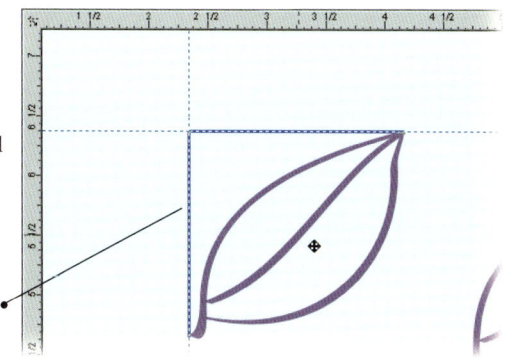

# STARTING TO DRAW

There are many tools for drawing in the CorelDRAW program, and countless means to achieve the effects you desire. In this chapter, we will try out some of the tools in the Curve flyout.

## DRAWING LINES AND OUTLINES

Drawing basic shapes is much easier with CorelDRAW than it appears. The program contains several tools to help you obtain the effect that you're trying to achieve. Incidentally, it is often easier to work on the page when it is zoomed to 400% or so.

### 1 DRAWING FREEHAND

- Select the **Freehand Tool** icon from the **Curve** flyout in the toolbox.
- Click on the page, hold down the left mouse button, and drag to draw.

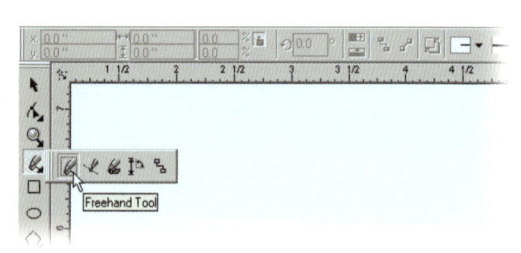

### NODES AND SHAPING HANDLES

Nodes are the square points at the end of a line or a segment of a curve. When a node is selected by clicking with the **Shape** tool, shaping handles appear. These can be dragged to alter the shape of the line.

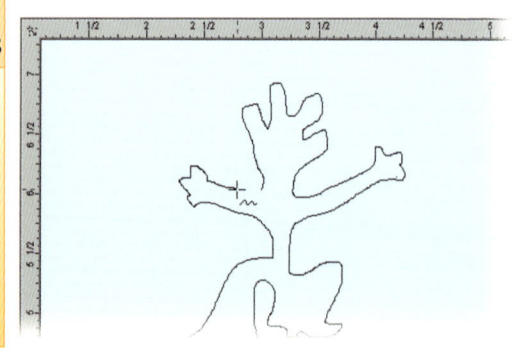

DRAWING LINES AND OUTLINES · 23

- Release the mouse button to see the result. The smoothing scale is set at 100, as shown in the illustration below. This setting has improved the quality of the lines, but much of the detail has been lost.

- To close the gap between the starting and ending nodes, click the **Auto-Close Curve** button in the property bar.

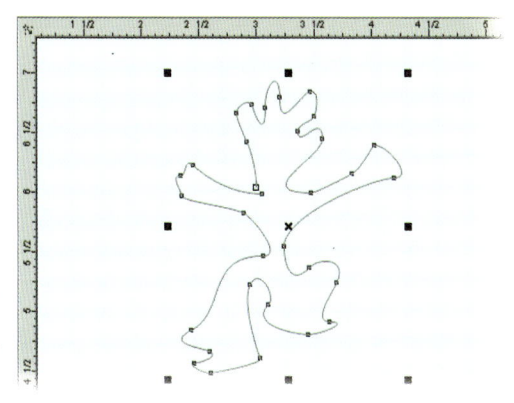

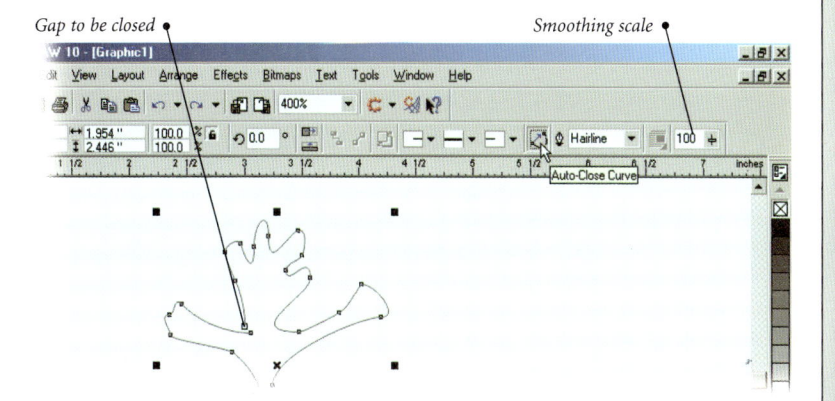

*Gap to be closed*

*Smoothing scale*

## 2 NODE EDITING

- Nodes can be added to the drawing or deleted. The best tool to manipulate nodes is the **Shape Tool**. Select it from the **Shape Edit** flyout in the toolbox.

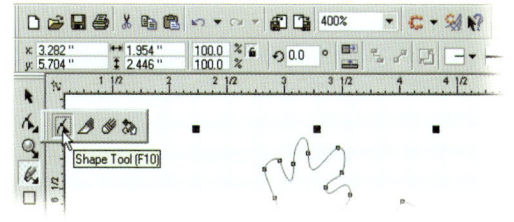

## 24 • STARTING TO DRAW

- To add a node, double-click on the outline of the object where you want the node to be positioned.
- Once a node has been added, the **Shape Tool** cursor appears, as it always does when the mouse cursor hovers over a node.

- Drag the nodes or use the shaping handles to curve the lines in a variety of ways.

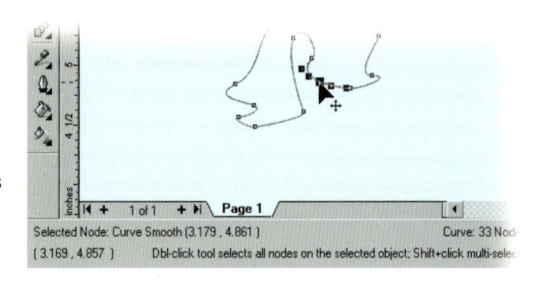

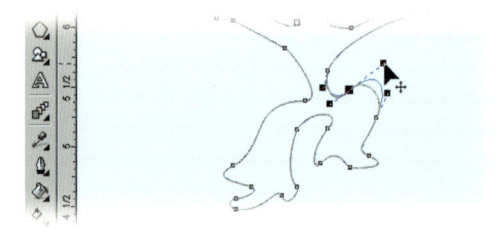

## 3 ADJUSTING THE LINE THICKNESS

- Using the **Pick Tool**, click on the object to select it, and then click on the down arrow of the **Outline Width** selector box on the property bar.

- Click on the required thickness. Here we have chosen **4.0pt** thickness.

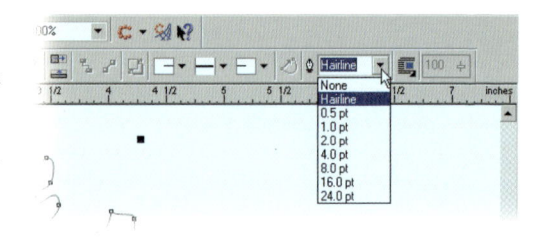

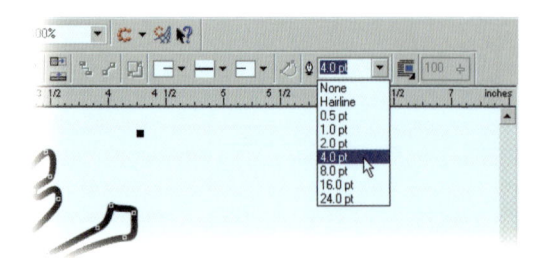

DRAWING LINES AND OUTLINES • 25

## 4 DRAWING WITH ARTISTIC MEDIA

- The **Artistic Media Tool** is capable of producing very dramatic effects.
- Select the **Artistic Media Tool** from the **Curve** flyout in the toolbox.

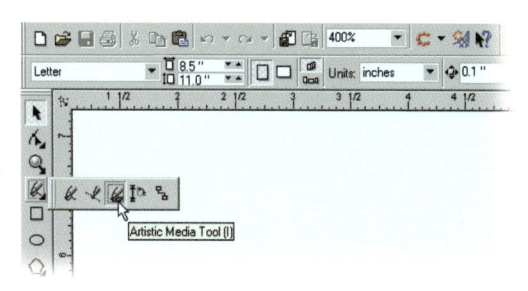

- Click on the **Brush** icon in the property bar.

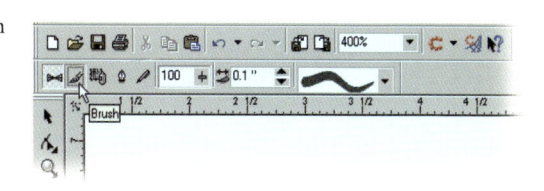

- Click on the down arrow next to the **Brush Stroke List** to see the drop-down menu of brush styles.

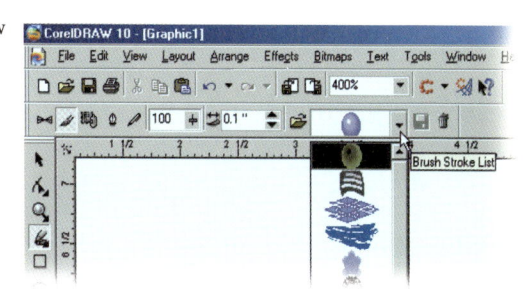

- Select one of the brush strokes. Here we are selecting **diamonds**.

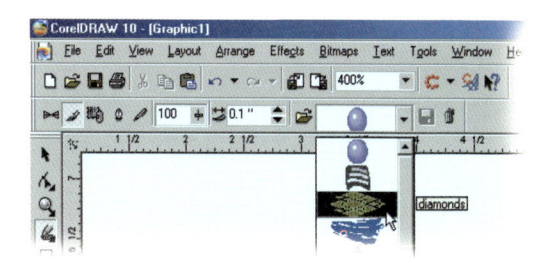

26 · STARTING TO DRAW

- Click on the page, hold down the left mouse button, and drag. Don't be alarmed by the thick black mark that appears.

- When you release the mouse button, your diamond brush strokes appear in place of your original mark.

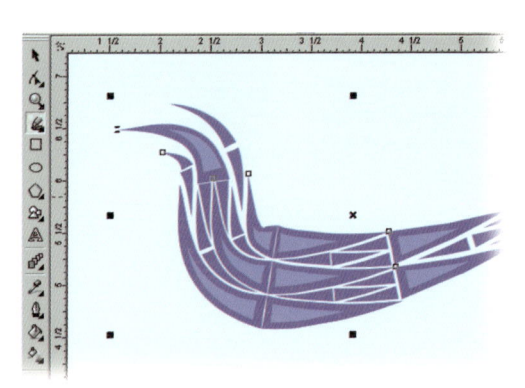

## 5 SPRAYING WITH ARTISTIC MEDIA

- Another effect created by the **Artistic Media Tool** is by the use of the **Sprayer**. Click on the **Sprayer** icon in the property bar.

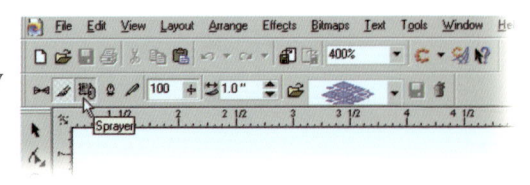

## DRAWING LINES AND OUTLINES · 27

- Click on the arrow of the **Spraylist File List** to view the drop-down menu.
- Select by clicking on one of the options. Here, we have selected **bubbles**.

- Click on the page and draw a line by dragging the **Sprayer** cursor with the mouse.
- The **Sprayer** will follow this line with the pattern you selected from the **Spraylist File List**. Release the mouse button to see the result.

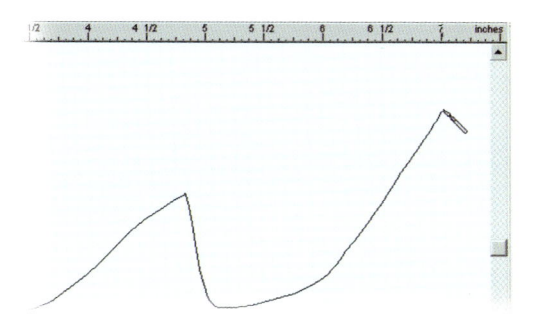

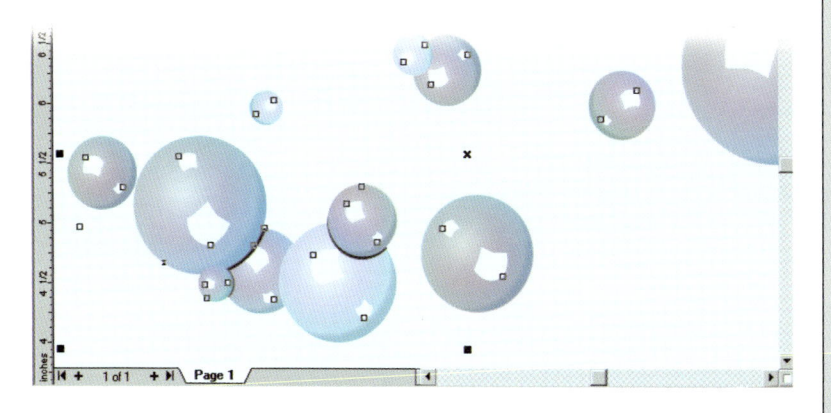

# DRAWING SHAPES

It is possible to draw a very wide range of shapes with CorelDRAW. An additional element in the program is the **Perfect Shapes** feature that allows quick access to 77 separate, customizable shapes via the toolbox and the property bar.

## 1 DRAWING RECTANGLES

● To draw a rectangle, click on the **Rectangle Tool** in the toolbox.

● Left-click your corner start position on the page, then drag the mouse until you have the desired size of rectangle before releasing the mouse button.

● If the rectangle needs to have specific dimensions, it is easier to draw a rectangle of any size first, then input the dimensions later.
● With the rectangle selected, highlight the **Object(s) Size** figure for width (the upper box), and type in the size you want. Do the same for the height (in the lower box) and press the [Enter ↵] key on your keyboard for the changes to take place.

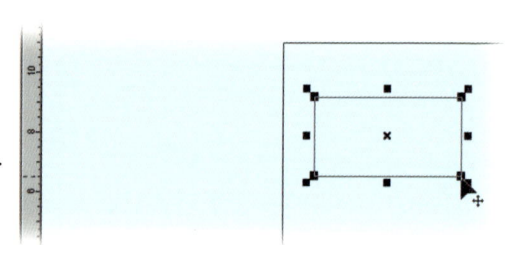

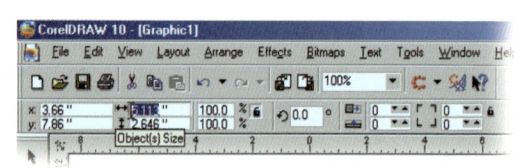

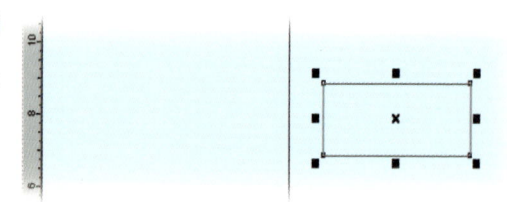

# DRAWING SHAPES · 29

## 2 ROUNDING THE CORNERS

- The corners of your rectangle or square can be rounded either separately or simultaneously. To increase the roundness of the corner at the top-right, use the **Right Rectangle Corner Roundness** up arrow in the property bar.

- To round all the corners simultaneously, first click on the **Round Corners Together** lock icon.
- Now, all the corners will be rounded by the number of increments selected for one corner. This also applies to any corner that has been previously rounded.
- With **Round Corners Together** deselected, the corners can be adjusted individually.

### QUICK SQUARES

A quick and simple way to draw a square is to click on the **Rectangle** tool in the toolbox, left-click the starting position, and hold down the [Ctrl] key on your keyboard as you drag.

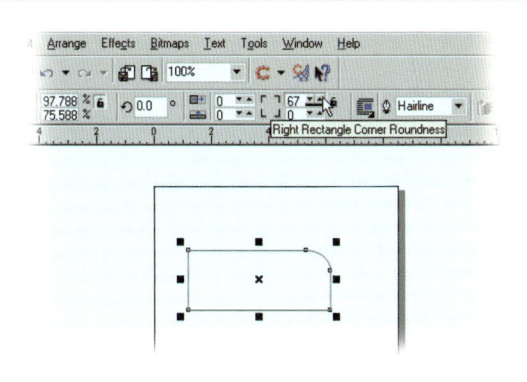

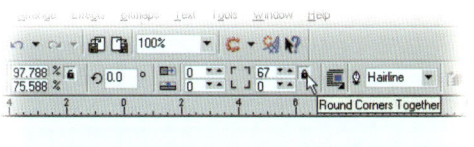

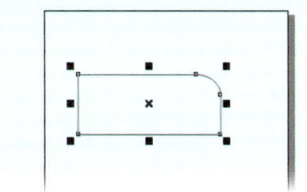

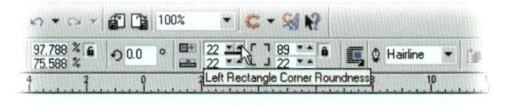

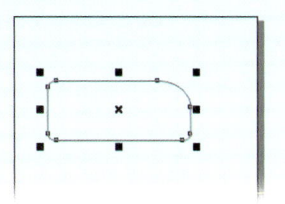

30 · STARTING TO DRAW

## 3 DRAWING ELLIPSES
- Click on the **Ellipse Tool** in the toolbox.
- Click on the page and, while holding down the left mouse button, drag the ellipse to the shape and size you want. Release the button when the required size has been reached.

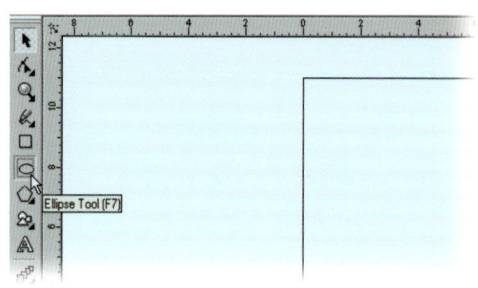

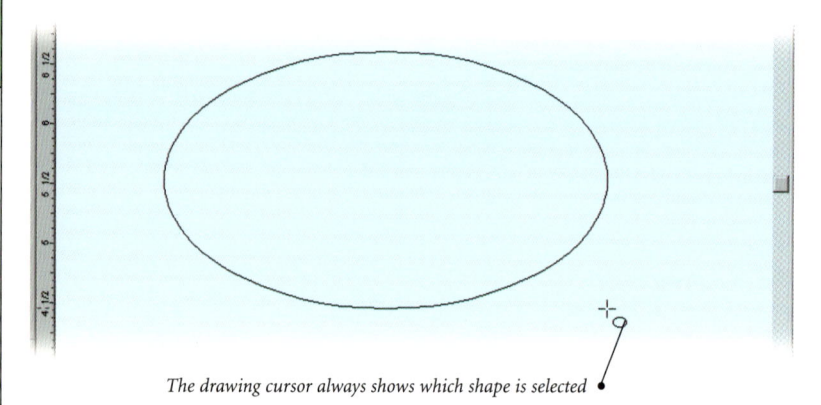

*The drawing cursor always shows which shape is selected*

## 4 CHANGING AN ELLIPSE TO A PIE
- With the ellipse selected, click on the **Pie** icon in the property bar.

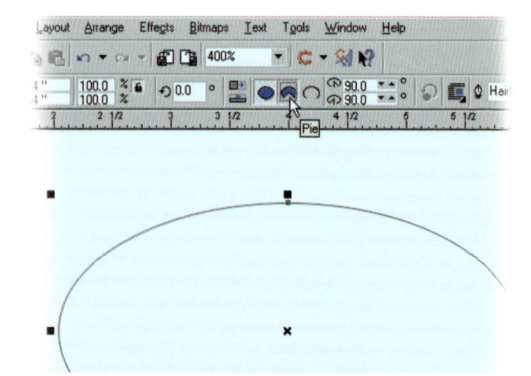

DRAWING SHAPES · 31

- The CorelDRAW default setting removes the bottom right corner to create the pie shape. Increase or decrease the size of the missing slice by using the arrows of the **Starting and Ending Angles** settings in the menu bar.

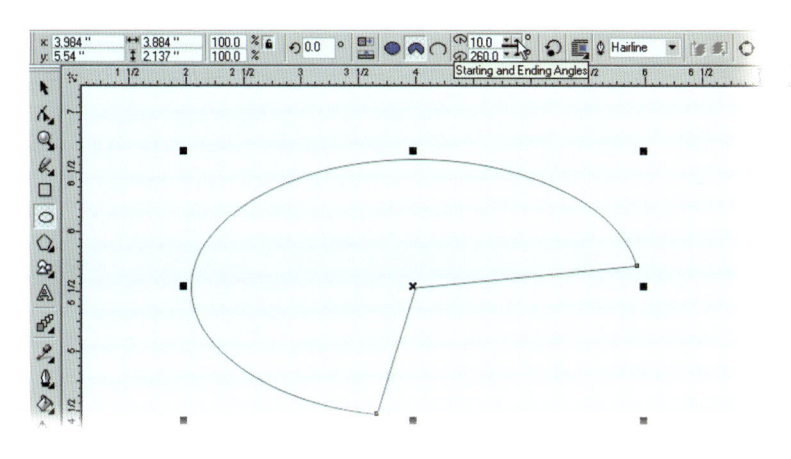

## 5 POLYGONS AND STARS

- Select the **Polygon Tool** from the **Object** flyout in the toolbox.

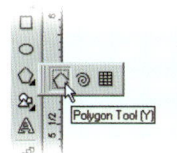

- Left-click on the page and drag to create your polygon. Release the mouse button when the polygon is the size you want.

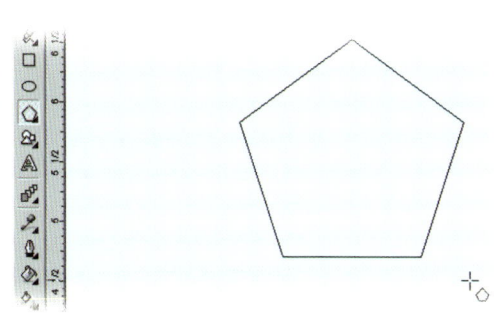

## 32 • STARTING TO DRAW

- The number of points on the polygon can be decreased or increased.
- Select the polygon and click on the spin buttons in the **Number of Points on Polygon** selector in the property bar.

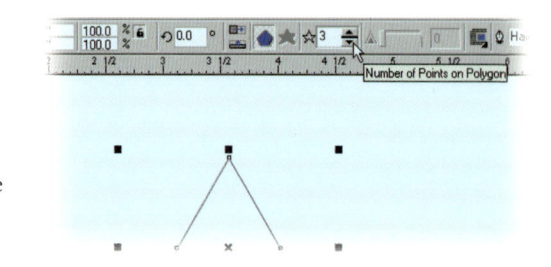

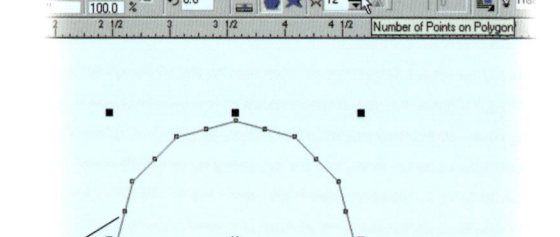

*Number of points on Polygon has been set to 12.*

- Click on the **Star** icon in the property bar for one of the possible types of star.
- With a polygon selected in the document, click on the **Star** icon to separate the polygon into two polygons – one superimposed on the other.

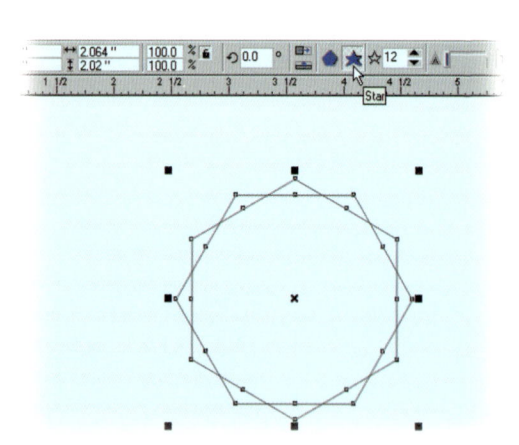

DRAWING SHAPES · 33

- Another way to create a star from a polygon is to click on any node on the outline of the polygon and drag inward toward the center.
- You can drag the line at an angle as we have done here, to create a spinning star effect.

- When you release the mouse button, the original outline of the polygon is removed to leave the star shape that you have created.

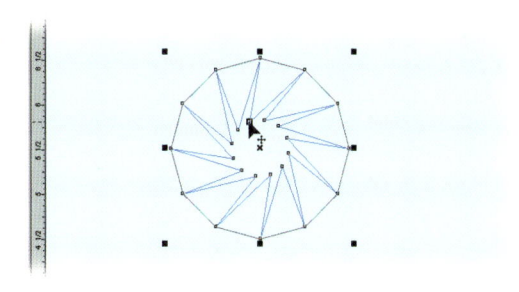

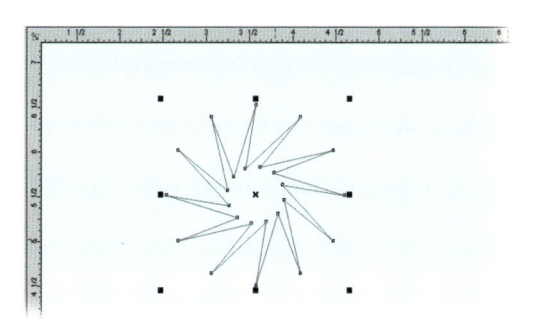

## 6 GENERATING SPIRALS

- Two types of spiral are available – symmetrical and logarithmic.
- From the **Object** flyout in the toolbox, select the **Spiral Tool**.

- Before drawing the spiral, choose the number of rings you want by using the arrows on the **Spiral Revolutions** selector in the property bar.

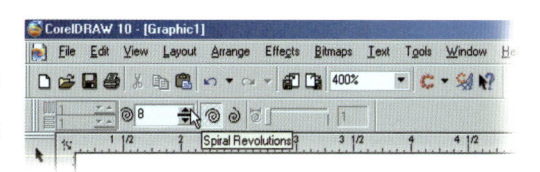

## 34 · STARTING TO DRAW

● Draw the two types of spiral by clicking on the page and dragging. First, with the **Symmetrical Spiral** icon selected, and then with the **Logarithmic Spiral** icon selected.

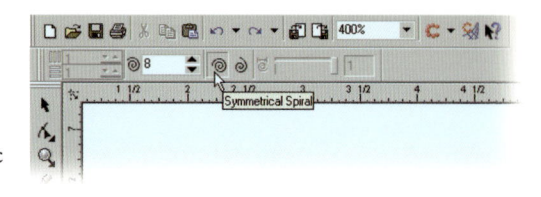

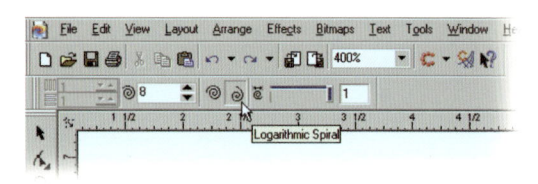

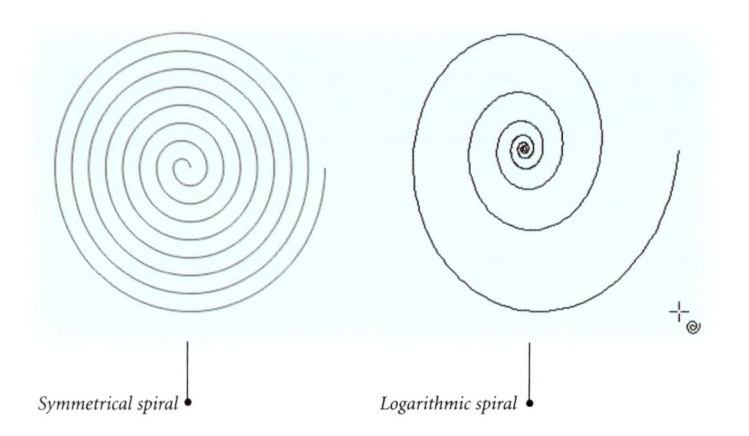

*Symmetrical spiral*

*Logarithmic spiral*

## 7 CHOOSING PRE-DEFINED SHAPES

● Open the **Perfect Shape** flyout from the toolbox by clicking on the corner triangle of the **Basic Shapes** icon.

DRAWING SHAPES · 35

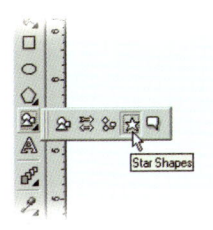

- From the flyout, select one of the categories of shapes. Here we are choosing **Star Shapes**.

- The **Perfect Shapes** star icon appears on the property bar. Click on it, and choose the shape you want to draw from the drop-down menu.

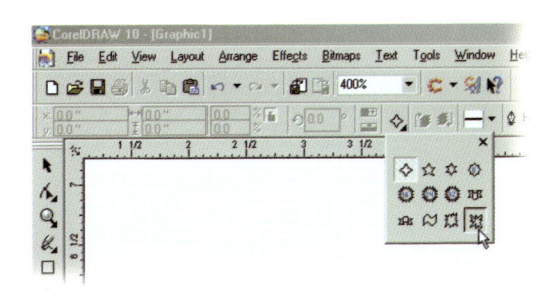

- This selection produces a star with a number of irregularly positioned points.
- Left-click on your page to start drawing and drag the shape to the desired size.
- Release the button to review the shape of your star.

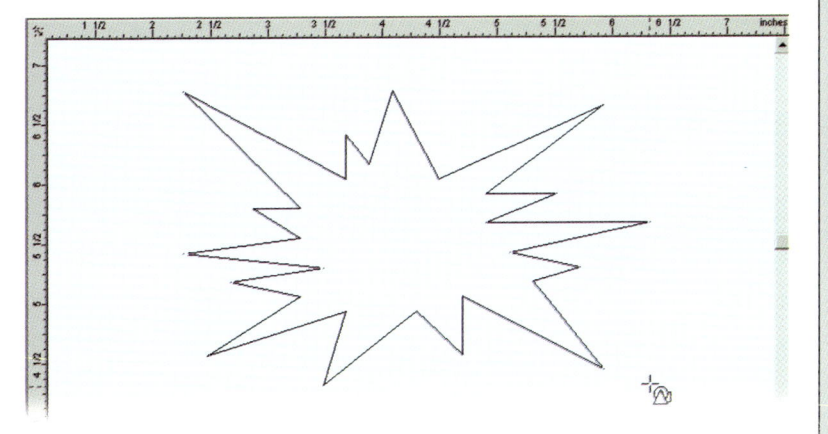

# HANDLING OBJECTS

**CorelDRAW offers almost limitless options for manipulating objects. In this chapter, we will look at some of the basic ways to transform and shape objects within a document.**

## TRANSFORMING OBJECTS

Once you have placed an object in a document, there are a number of ways to manipulate it with CorelDRAW. This manipulation, known as transforming, can be achieved by mirroring, skewing in any direction, or by rotation.

### 1 MIRRORING OBJECTS

● To mirror this arrow, which was created from the **Perfect Shapes** flyout in the toolbox, click on it to select.
● Then, click on one of the mirror buttons in the property bar. Here, the horizontal option of the **Mirror Buttons** has been selected.

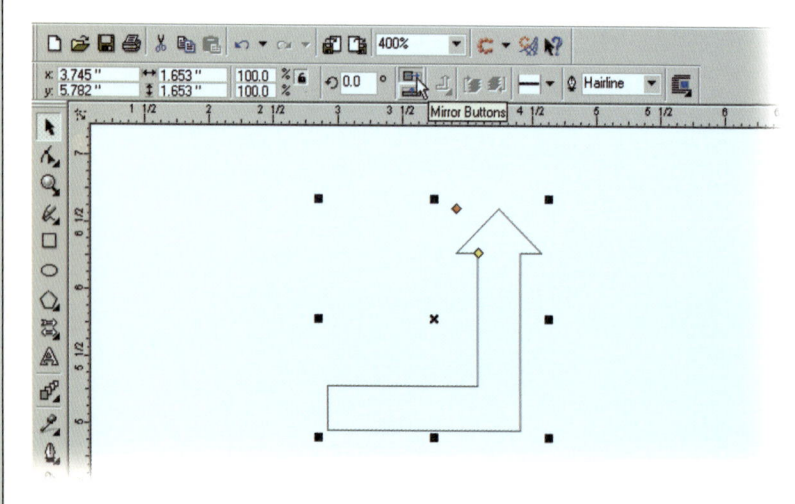

# TRANSFORMING OBJECTS · 37

## USING THE PICK TOOL AND SELECTING OBJECTS

- The **Pick Tool** is undoubtedly the most used tool in the toolbox. To move or apply any effect or transformation to an object, text, or guideline, you first need to use the **Pick Tool**.
- Select any object – artistic text, text frame, or guideline with a single click of the **Pick Tool**.
- A selected item will have selection handles.
- A selected guideline is in a different color from an unselected one.
- To select a group of objects, click and drag a rectangle around them with the **Pick Tool**. All the objects within that rectangle will be selected and any transformations made will apply to each of the objects.
- To select more than one object from a group while leaving the rest of the group unselected, hold down the `Shift` key as you click on each object.
- To select all instances of one category of items in your document, click on **Edit** in the menu bar, then choose **Select All** from the drop-down menu that appears, and then either **Objects**, **Text**, or **Guidelines**.

## 2 SKEWING OBJECTS

- The arrow has now been mirrored horizontally. To skew the angles of an object, double-click on the object. This will change the selection handles to skewing handles.
- Move your cursor over one of the skewing handles.

*Cursor over a skewing handle*

- Click and drag to skew the object. An outline appears on-screen to show how the skewed object will look.

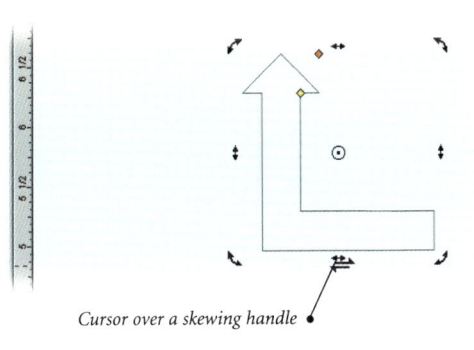

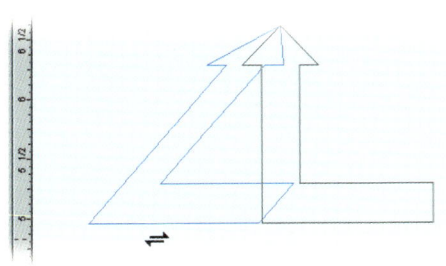

## 3 ROTATING OBJECTS

- Releasing the button produces the newly skewed shape. To rotate the object around its center point, first double-click on the object.
- Next, instead of dragging one of the side skewing handles, click on one of the curved corner skewing handles.

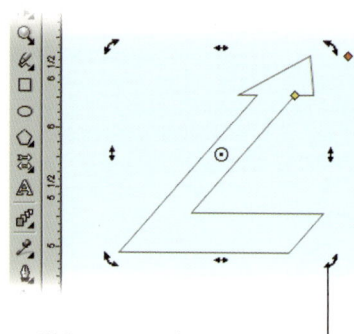

*Click on any one of the corner handles*

- The rotation cursor now appears, and you can drag and rotate the object as required. Again, an outline shape appears showing how far the object has been rotated. The bull's-eye shows the center of rotation around which the object turns.

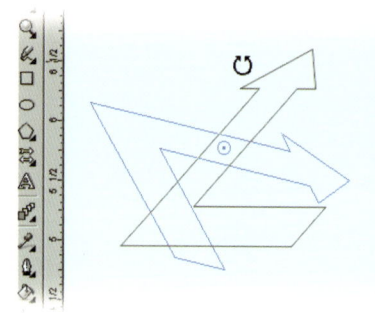

- Release the mouse button when the required degree of rotation has been reached.

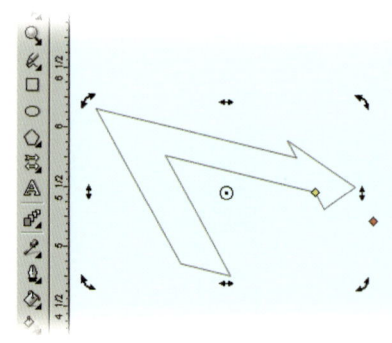

# Shaping Objects

Overlapping two shapes can create a pleasing third shape. One object can trim another so only part of it remains visible; the shapes can join each other to become a single shape, or the shape created by an overlap can become a separate object.

## 1 TRIMMING AN OBJECT

- We will use the **Trim** option to create a flash for an ellipse.
- Using the **Ellipse** tool from the toolbox, draw an ellipse □.

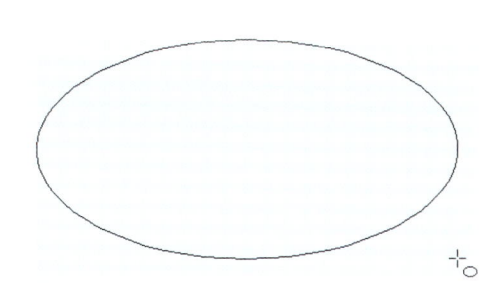

- Duplicate the ellipse by selecting it with the **Pick Tool**, left-click on the outline, drag it to the new location, click the right mouse button and release the left mouse button.
- Arrange the ellipses so they overlap as shown.

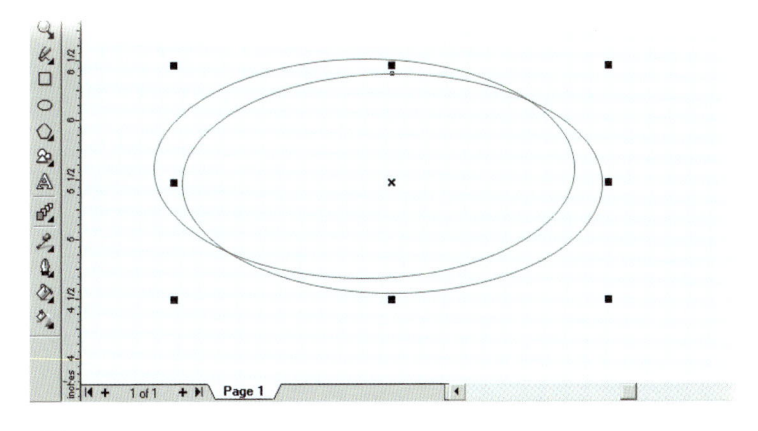

Drawing Ellipses

## 40 · HANDLING OBJECTS

- Select the lower ellipse, click on **Arrange** in the menu bar, and choose **Shaping** from the drop-down menu. In the submenu that appears, select **Trim** from the three options.

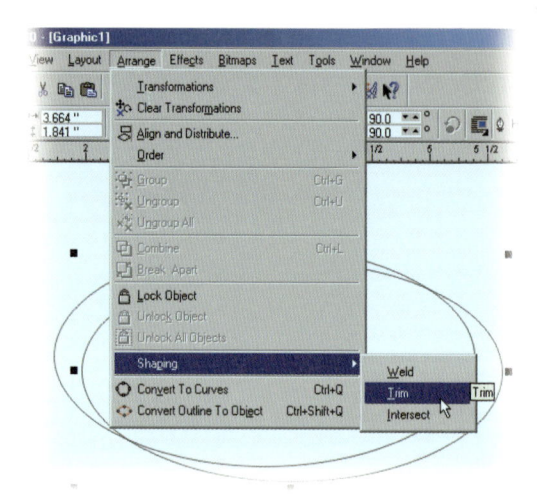

- The **Shaping** docker appears with the **Trim** option selected.
- We want the lower ellipse (the source) to remain as it is, and the second ellipse (the target) to be trimmed, so that the part that is not overlapped is all that remains. For this to happen, make sure that the **Source Object(s)** box that appears under the **Leave Original** options is checked.
- With that box checked, click on **Trim**.

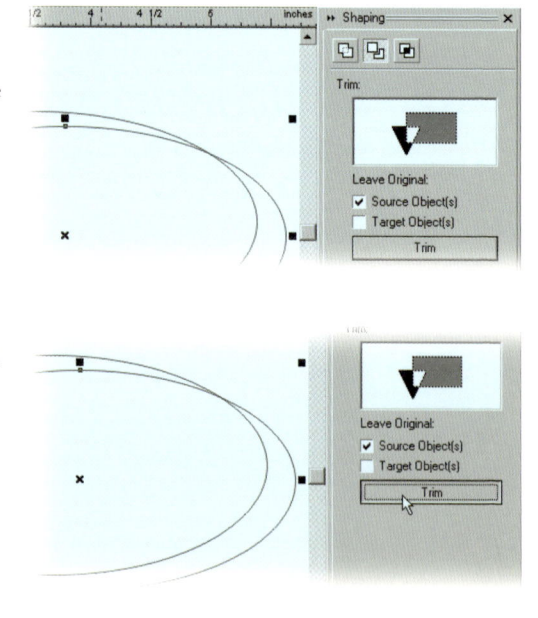

SHAPING OBJECTS · 41

- Place the cursor over the target ellipse and left-click on it.

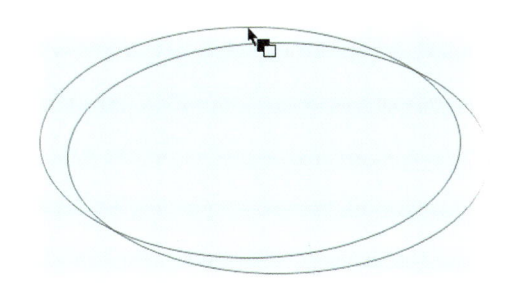

- You now have the lower ellipse remaining, plus the trimmed section of the upper ellipse.
- Shrink the trimmed section by selecting it with the **Pick Tool** and dragging it to size.

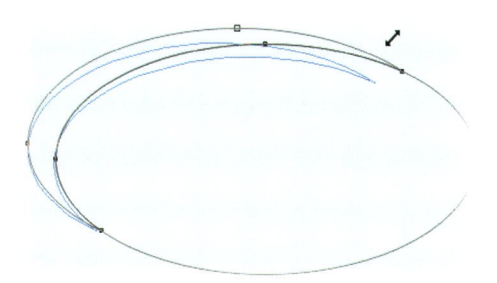

- Position the trimmed flash on the remaining, complete ellipse.

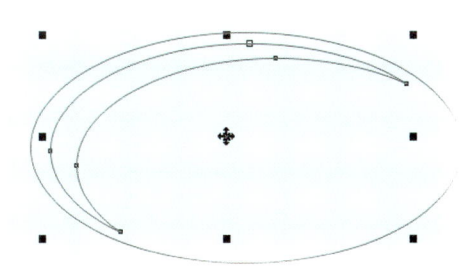

## 42 · HANDLING OBJECTS

## 2 WELDING OBJECTS

- Several drawing objects can be turned into one object by welding them together. Here, a collection of circles has been selected with the exception of the central, red circle. The other circles will be welded to this red circle.

- Go to the menu bar, click on **Arrange** and select **Shaping** from the drop-down menu, then **Weld** from the submenu.

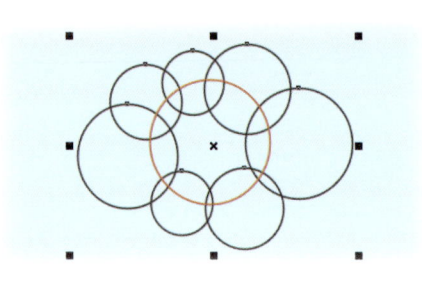

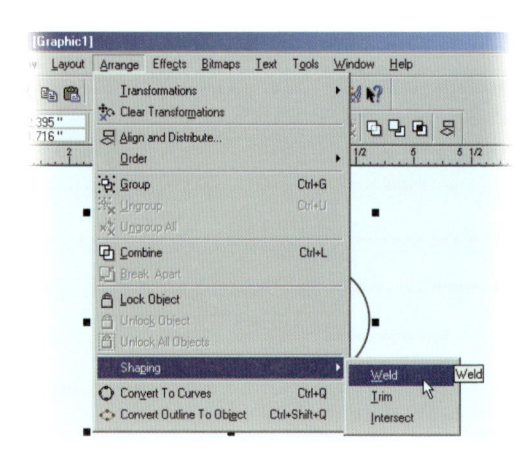

- The **Shaping** docker opens with **Weld** selected.
- With both the **Source Object(s)** and the **Target Object(s)** boxes unchecked, click on the **Weld To** button.

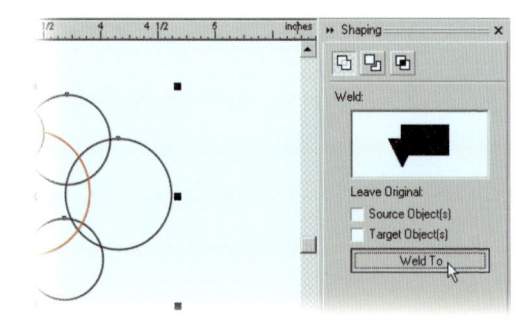

SHAPING OBJECTS • 43

- The cursor has changed to the distinctive weld cursor. Click on the central circle to see the new shape. The qualities of the central circle (to which the others are welded) are applied to the final shape – color of outline, fill, and thickness of line.

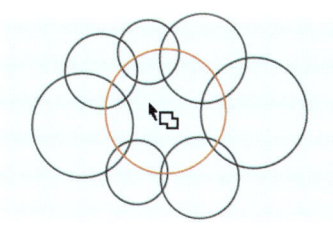

- The new shape appears. This method can be used to create any number of irregular and nonstandard shapes. Once a collection of objects has been welded together, they can be treated as a single object. Any changes that you make, such as color, shape, size, or effects, are applied equally to every element in the object.

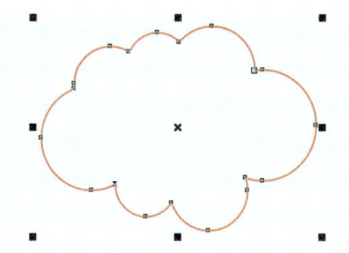

- The possible uses for new shapes are only limited by your imagination.

## 44 • HANDLING OBJECTS

## 3 INTERSECTING SHAPES

- The two shapes we have here, the rectangle and the star, will be used to create a third shape based on the overlap of the two.
- Select one of the shapes. Here, we have selected the star with the **Pick Tool** from the toolbox.

- Go to the menu bar and click on **Arrange**. Choose **Shaping** from the drop-down menu and then select **Intersect** from the submenu. This will open the **Shaping** docker.

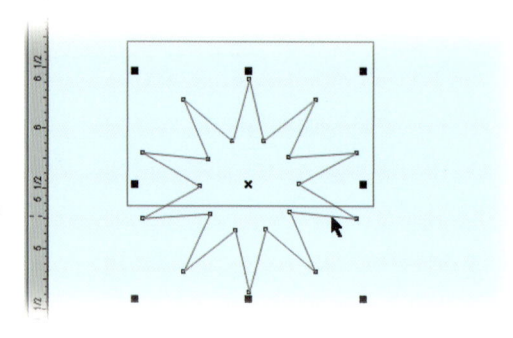

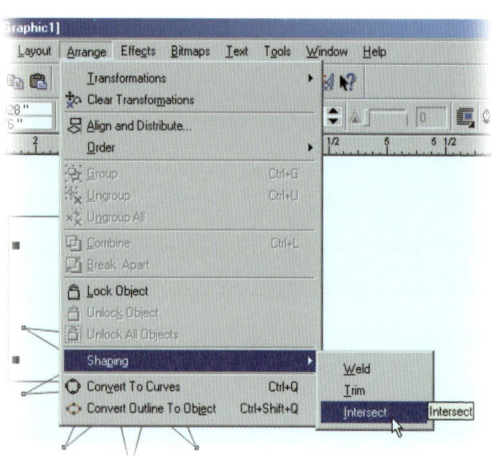

- The shape selected, the star, is the source object. To retain it after the intersection takes place, check the **Source Object(s)** box. To keep the rectangle – the target object – check the **Target Object(s)** box. To remove both complete shapes after the intersection, uncheck both boxes as here.

| 28 | **Drawing Rectangles** | 31 | **Polygons and Stars** |

SHAPING OBJECTS · 45

- Click on the **Intersect With** button.

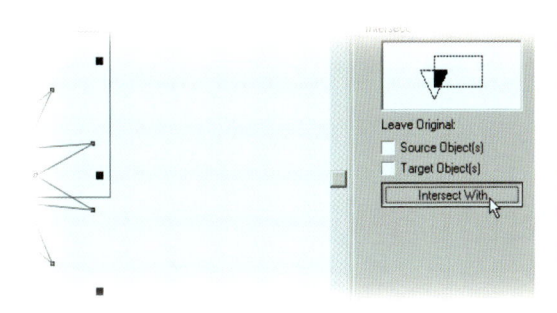

- The cursor changes to the intersect cursor.
- Select the rectangle by clicking on it.

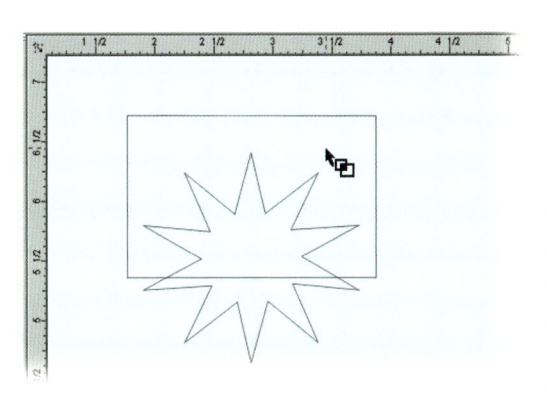

- As you click on the rectangle, its outline is removed. The area of the star within the rectangle remains to create the third shape, from the intersection of the original two.

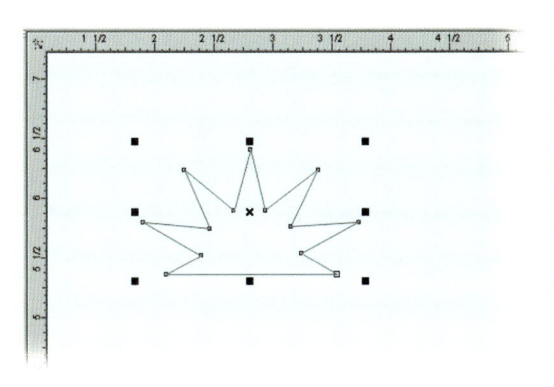

# WORKING WITH TEXT

CorelDRAW's text handling is very impressive. In this chapter, we will show you how text can be shaped, fitted to paths, wrapped around objects, and filled with color and textures.

## USING ARTISTIC TEXT

There are four different types of text in CorelDRAW 10 – stand-alone artistic text, stand-alone paragraph text, text on a path, and text within a shape. Here, we will concentrate on artistic text; the default font is AvantGarde, 24pt.

### 1 ADDING ARTISTIC TEXT
- Click on the **Text Tool** in the toolbox. Then click on the page where you want to start your text.
- Type in your wording on the page.

### 2 CHOOSING A NEW FONT
- Before making any changes to the font, choose the **Pick Tool** from the toolbox. The text will show as being selected.

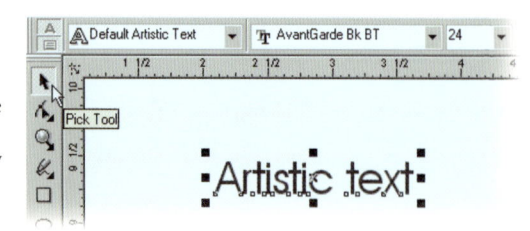

USING ARTISTIC TEXT • 47

- Choose a font from the **Font List** drop-down menu in the property bar. You can see a display of how the selected text will look in each font style. Here, **Brush738 BT** has been selected.

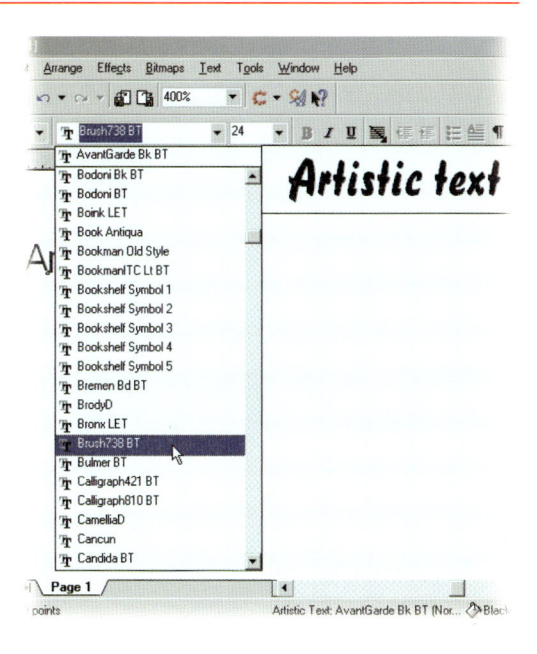

- Choose the font size from the **Font Size List** in the property bar.

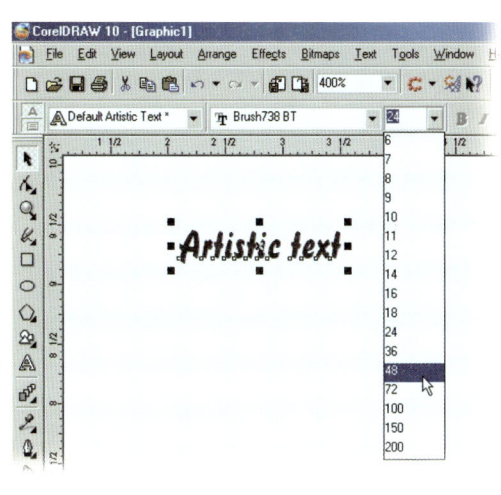

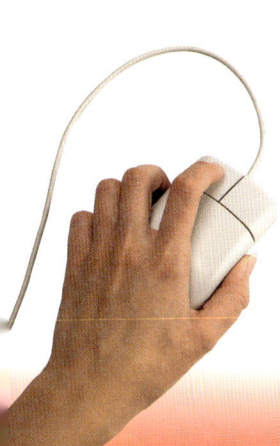

# SHAPING ARTISTIC TEXT

Applying an envelope to artistic text is a way of changing its shape. No matter how you change the envelope, the text will change to fit it. You can also also manipulate your text to make it follow a path to produce different effects.

## 1 SHAPING TEXT USING ENVELOPES

- To open the **Envelope Docker Window**, click on **Effects** in the menu bar, and then **Envelope**.

- Select your text with the **Pick Tool**, and click on **Add Preset** in the **Envelope** docker window, to choose from a variety of preset envelopes.

- Select one of the shapes and click on the **Apply** button.

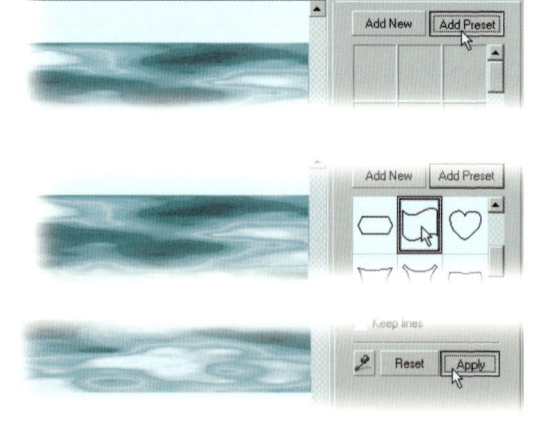

## SHAPING ARTISTIC TEXT • 49

- If you need to undo the envelope effect, click on **Effects** in the menu bar and select **Clear Envelope** from the drop-down menu.

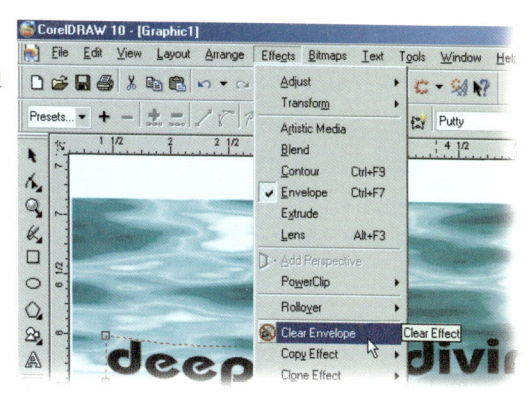

- To apply a custom envelope, click on **Add New** in the **Envelope** docker window.

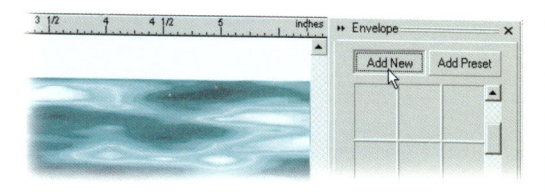

- A rectangular envelope with nodes appears around the selected text.

- Use these nodes to customize the envelope and pull it into the shape you want. You will see that the text instantly changes its shape.

## 50 • WORKING WITH TEXT

### 2 FITTING TEXT TO A PATH

- You may have a text string, as has been typed in here, which you want to follow a shaped path.
- Through the bubbles, which were created with the **Artistic Media** tool, draw a freehand path, with the **Freehand Tool** from the **Curve** flyout of the toolbox.

- With the path still selected, click on the **Pick Tool** in the toolbox, and, while holding down the ⇧Shift key on your keyboard, select the text. Now both the text and the path are selected.

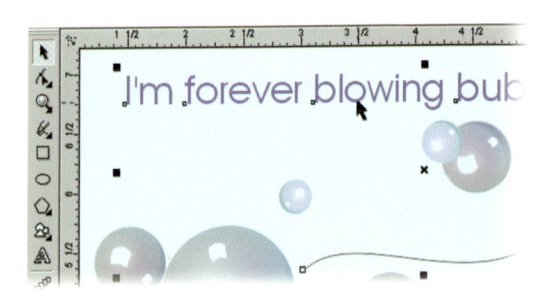

- Go to the menu bar and click on **Text**. Then select **Fit Text To Path** from the drop-down menu.

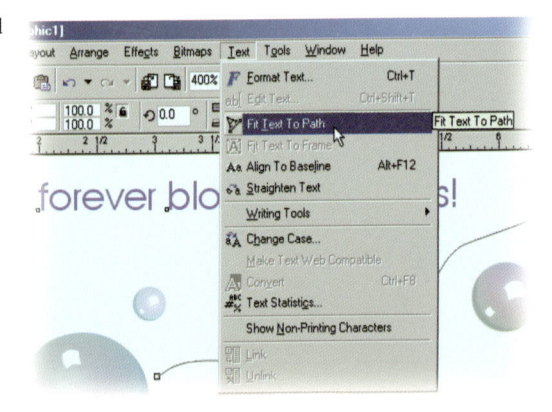

**Spraying With Artistic Media** 26

# SHAPING ARTISTIC TEXT · 51

- The line of text now follows the curved path.

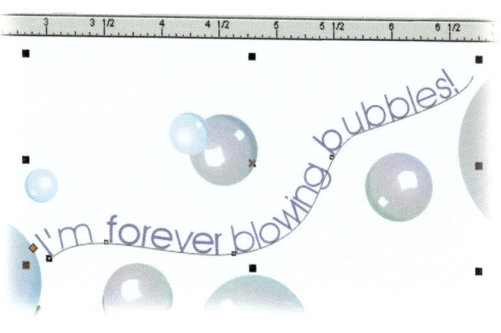

- Click away from the text and the path with the **Pick Tool**. Then click back on the path.

- Press the Delete key on your keyboard to remove the path.

# USING PARAGRAPH TEXT

Using paragraph text is like placing a small word processor in your document. The text is placed in frames and can flow from one frame to another. Any objects placed inside or overlapping a text frame can be wrapped by the text.

## 1 ADDING PARAGRAPH TEXT

- Select the **Text Tool** from the toolbox.

- Click on the page and drag to create a text frame.

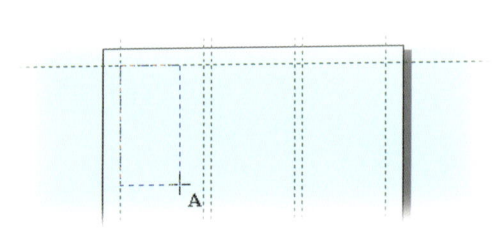

- Here we are fitting three text frames into the columns created by the guidelines preset, **Three Column Newsletter**.
- We are going to paste an extract from *Walden & On the Duty of Civil Disobedience* by Henry Thoreau, downloaded from a website. With the **Text Tool** still selected, click inside one of the text frames, then click on the **Paste** button in the standard toolbar to paste the text in.

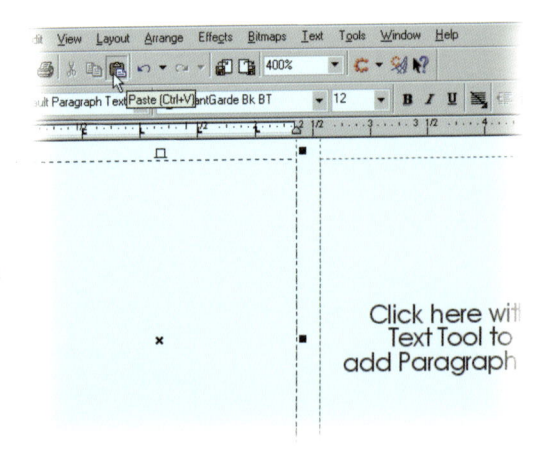

**Applying Preset Guidelines** 19

## USING PARAGRAPH TEXT · 53

## 2 CHOOSING A FONT
- Once the text is pasted in, you can apply a different font to a whole text frame.
- Select the frame with the **Pick Tool** and choose a font from the **Font List** in the property bar. **Viner Hand ITC** has been selected here.

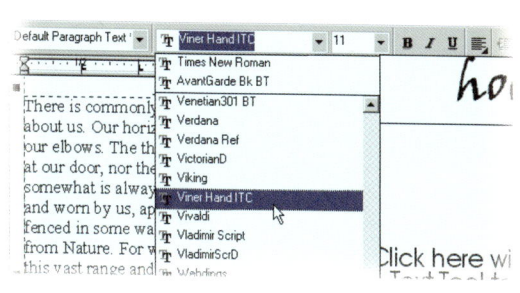

## 3 FLOWING PARAGRAPH TEXT
- To flow the text from one text frame to another, first click on the rectangle, which indicates overflowing text, at the base of the selected text frame.

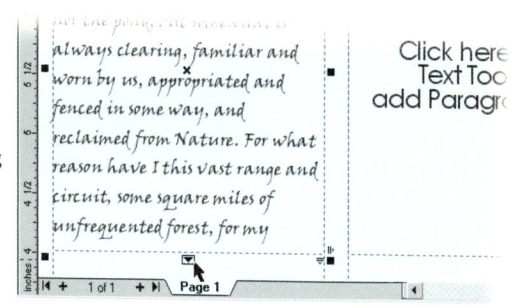

- When you move the cursor over another text frame, the cursor becomes a large black arrow.
- Click the arrow in the text frame into which you want your text to flow. Repeat these steps for each subsequent text frame.

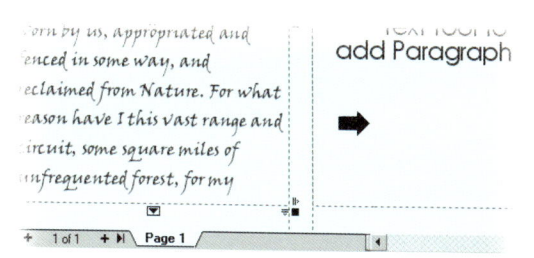

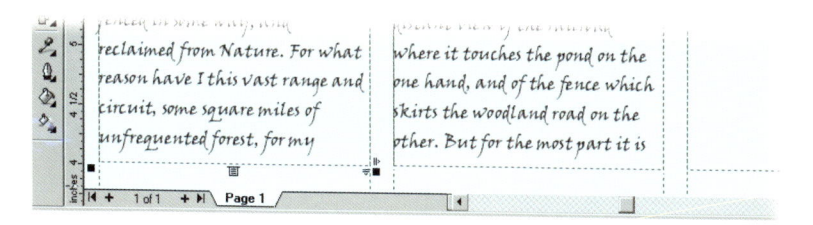

## 4. WRAPPING PARAGRAPH TEXT

- To illustrate this piece of text, we have imported a piece of clipart from the CorelDRAW Clipart Disc, which is part of the CorelDRAW package.

- To wrap the text around the image, click on the **Wrap Paragraph Text** icon in the property bar to view the options in its drop-down menu.

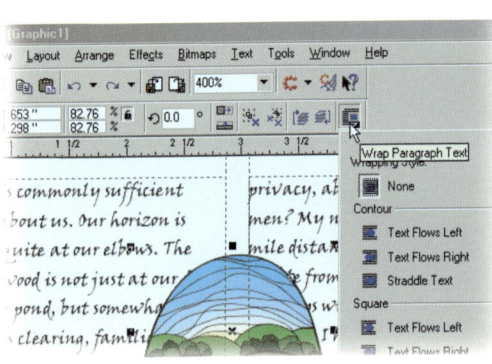

---

### LABELED TEXT FRAMES

- When text frames are first positioned they have no text inside them. If we zoom in to them, we see them clearly labeled with a reminder that they are text frames awaiting text.

- This is an automatic feature of CorelDRAW, and it is very useful because without this indication, the text frames would be completely invisible when precisely aligned with guidelines.

## USING PARAGRAPH TEXT • 55

● Here, we have selected the **Square, Straddle Text** option. Click on **OK** to apply the option.

● If you need to, you can adjust the alignment of a text frame by selecting the frame with the **Pick Tool**, clicking on the top of the frame and dragging.

● Eventually, your text should wrap squarely around the image.

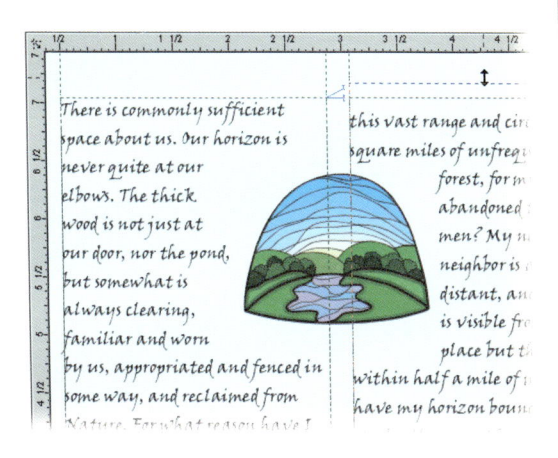

---

### IMPORTING CLIPART

● To import clipart, insert the CD-ROM and click on **File** in the menu bar, then select **Import**.

● Select the **Clipart CD** from the **Look In** selector. Double-click on the folders until you reach the clipart in the category that you want.

● To preview your choices, make sure the **Preview** box is checked as you click on each image.

● When the clipart you want is displayed in the preview area, click on **Import**, then drag on the clipart with the cursor to resize and position the image.

# FILLS AND COLORS

Once you have drawn your objects or created your text, you will be ready to apply fills. You can choose from uniform colors or from a vast array of special fills.

## APPLYING A UNIFORM FILL

Uniform fills are flat colors. The easiest way to apply a uniform fill to an object or text is to use the palette at the right-hand side of the screen. This is the **Default CMYK palette**, and it provides a good selection of colors for instant access.

### USING THE DEFAULT CMYK PALETTE
- Here, a shape has been drawn and that is to be filled.
- Open the **Default CMYK palette** by clicking on the arrow at the base of the palette.

- The palette opens to show you the selection of available colors.

*Color mix*
CMYK colors are colors made up from a mixture of cyan, magenta, yellow, and black.

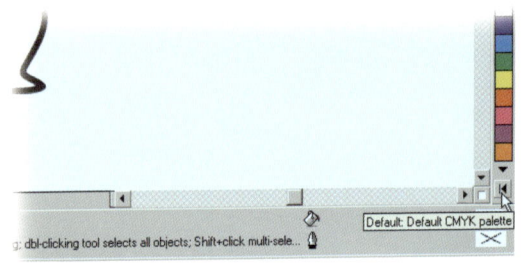

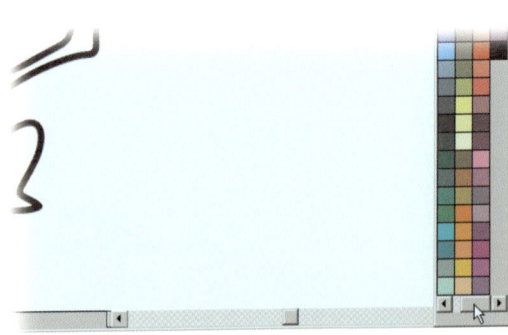

APPLYING SPECIAL FILLS • 57

- With the object selected, left-click on any of the colors in the palette to fill the object with that color.

- To color the outline, right-click any color in the palette.

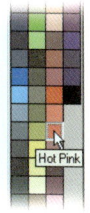

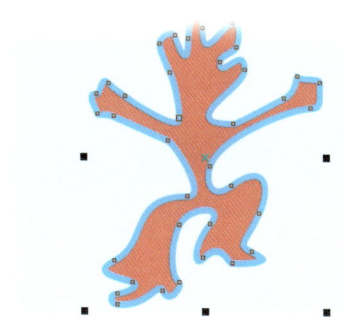

## APPLYING SPECIAL FILLS

Special fills can be applied to objects and text. They include fountain fills, where two or more colors blend into one another, and texture fills, which allow an almost infinite variety of visual textures to be applied within your documents.

### 1 APPLYING A FOUNTAIN FILL

- To fill an object with a fountain fill, first select the object with the **Pick Tool**.
- From the **Fill** flyout in the toolbox, select **Fountain Fill Dialog**.

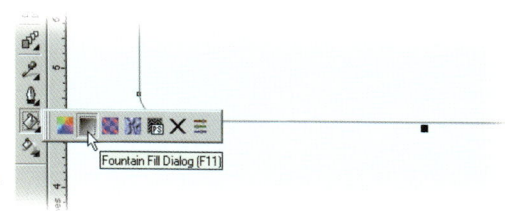

# 58 · FILLS AND COLORS

- This opens the **Fountain Fill** dialog box. There are four types of fountain fill: **Linear**, **Radial**, **Conical**, and **Square**.
- A **Linear** fountain fill flows in a straight line across the object. A **Radial** fill radiates from the center of the object. A **Conical** fountain fill circles from the center of the object giving the impression of an aerial view of a cone. A **Square** fountain fill radiates in concentric squares from the center of the object.

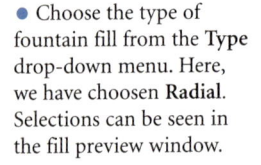

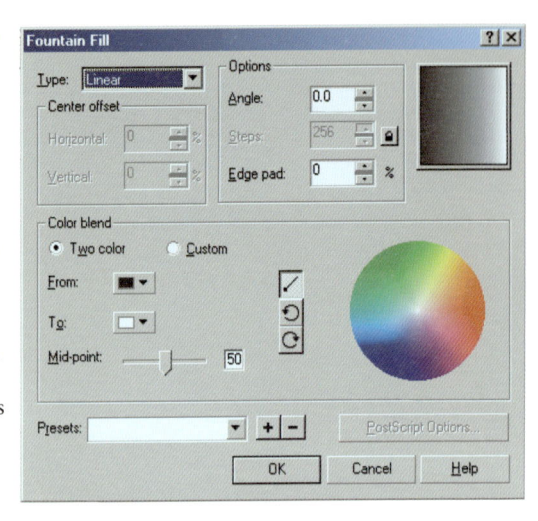

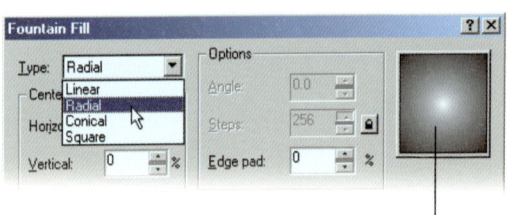

- Choose the type of fountain fill from the **Type** drop-down menu. Here, we have choosen **Radial**. Selections can be seen in the fill preview window.

*Fill preview window*

- To move the center point from which the fill is to radiate, use the spin buttons of the **Center offset** selector. The results again are shown in the preview window to the right.
- You can also click and drag inside the preview window to move the center point.

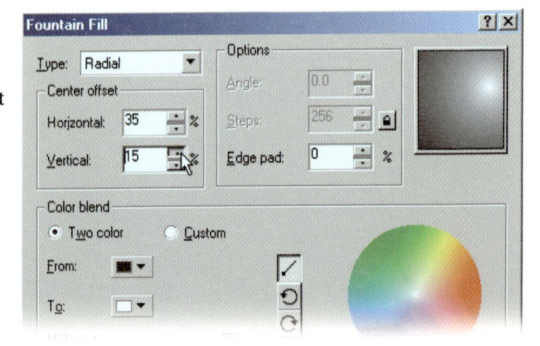

## APPLYING SPECIAL FILLS · 59

- Next, choose your colors from the **Color blend** drop-down menu.

- When you are happy with the effect in the preview window, click on **OK**.

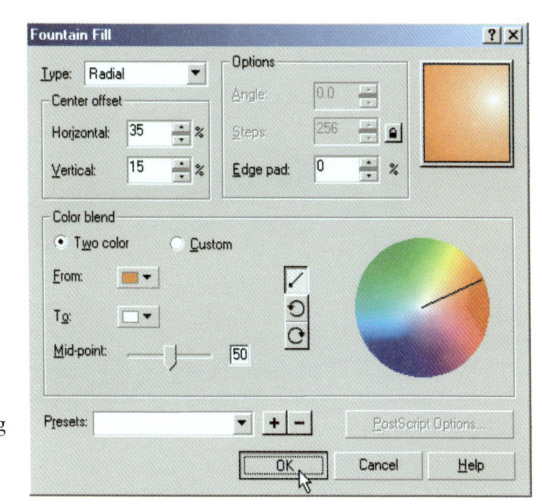

- The **Fountain Fill** dialog box closes and the object is filled.

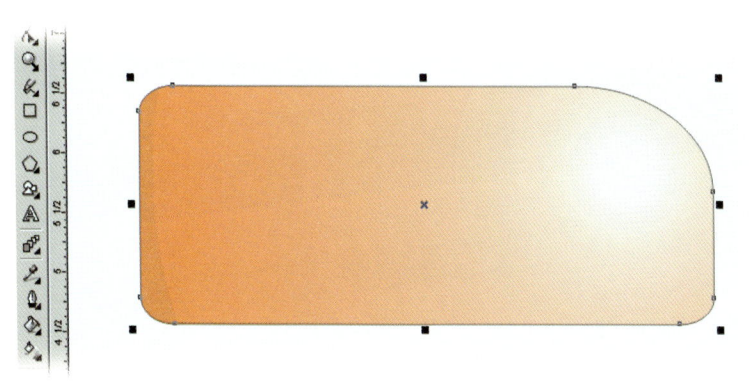

## 60 · FILLS AND COLORS

## 2 APPLYING A TEXTURE FILL

- With your object selected, in this case text, click on **Texture Fill Dialog** from the **Fill** flyout in the toolbox.

- The **Texture Fill** dialog box opens, and one of the many preset fills is displayed in the **Preview** window.

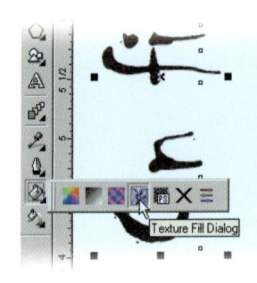

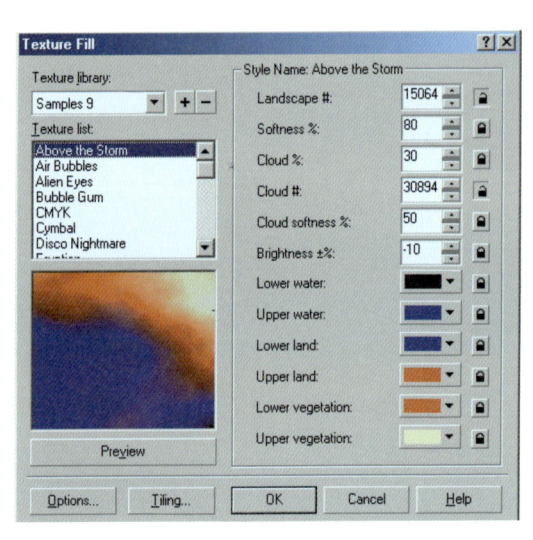

- Click on each name in the **Texture list** to see the fill displayed in the preview window.

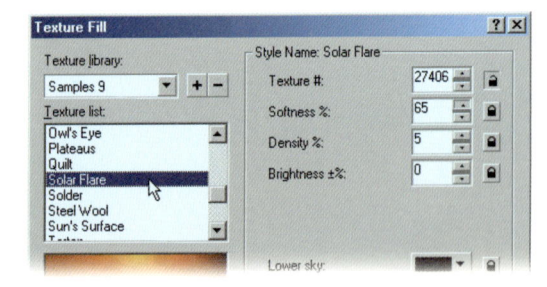

APPLYING SPECIAL FILLS · 61

- When you are happy with your selection, click on **OK**.

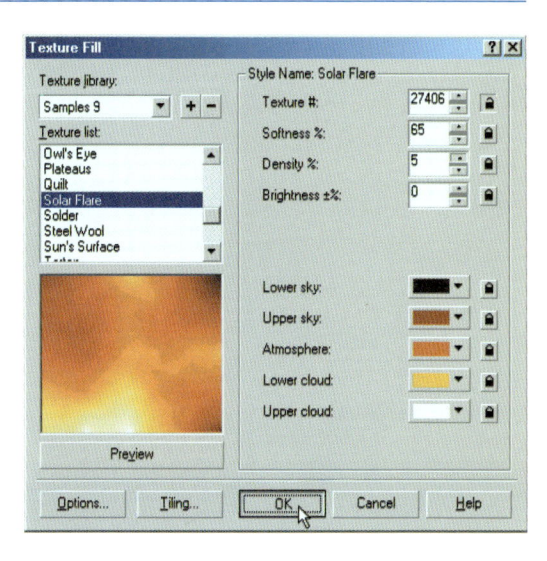

- Click off the text to remove the selection handles and view the result.

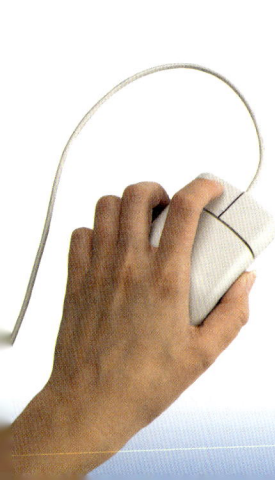

# 3-D EFFECTS

**Adding a third dimension to your objects and drawings is the single most effective way of bringing them to life and giving them substance. The important point is not to overdo it.**

## CREATING 3-D EFFECTS

To give the impression of an object or a piece of text disappearing into the distance, we can add perspective. Blending colors can make an object appear to be reflecting light from its rounded surface. Adding a drop shadow adds depth, and extruding a flat object gives that object a very convincing third dimension.

### 1 ADDING PERSPECTIVE

- Use the **Pick Tool** to select the object – text in this case – and click on **Effects** in the menu bar. In the drop-down menu, select **Add Perspective**.
- Drag any corner of the grid to give the illusion of perspective. The word **Goodbye** has been made to recede into the distance.

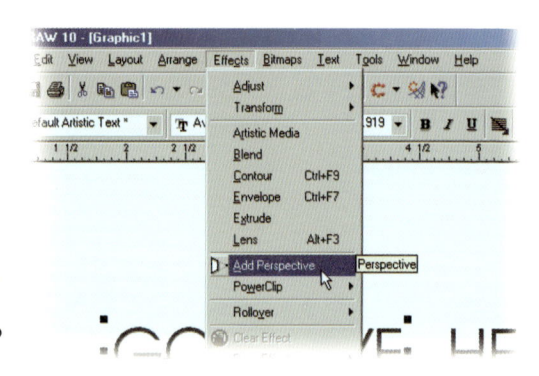

CREATING 3-D EFFECTS · 63

- Pulling the end of the word **Hello** gives the impression of the word emerging out of the page.

- Click on the **Pick Tool** to remove the grid, and click off the text to see the results.

## 2 USING THE BLEND TOOL

- We are now going to give the ellipse, containing the flash, the appearance of a three-dimensional object by blending the flash into the ellipse.
- First, we apply colors to the ellipse and the flash.
- Now, with both objects selected, click on the **Interactive Blend Tool** icon from the **Interactive Tool** flyout in the toolbox.

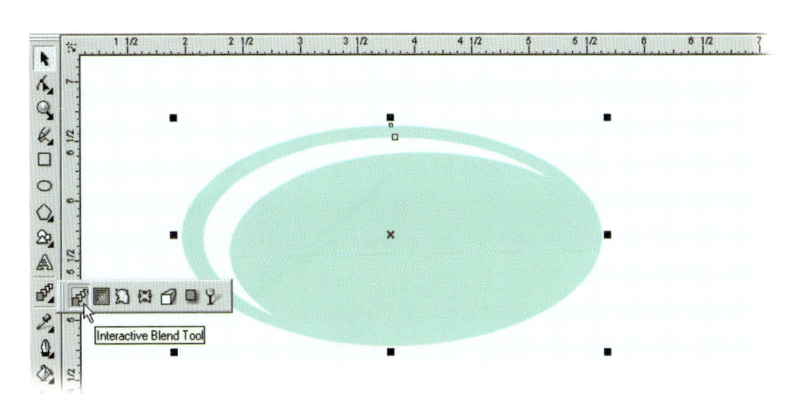

| 39 | **Trimming an Object** |
| 56 | **Applying a Uniform Fill** |

## 64 • 3-D EFFECTS

- Click on one object and drag to the other. The lines that appear indicate each step that is being made in the blend.

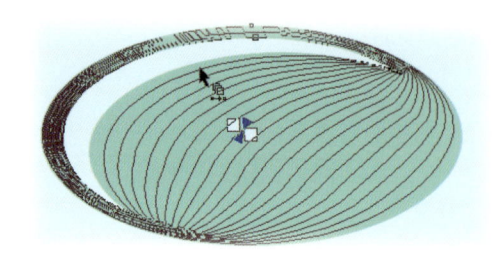

- The default number of steps is 20. You can alter this number before or after applying the blend.

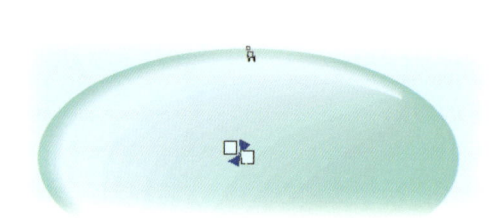

- Increase or decrease the number of steps by using the **Offset Between Blend Shapes** spin buttons in the property bar.
- Here, we are reducing the number of steps to 5.

- Select the **Pick Tool** and click on the page away from the blended objects to complete the transformation.

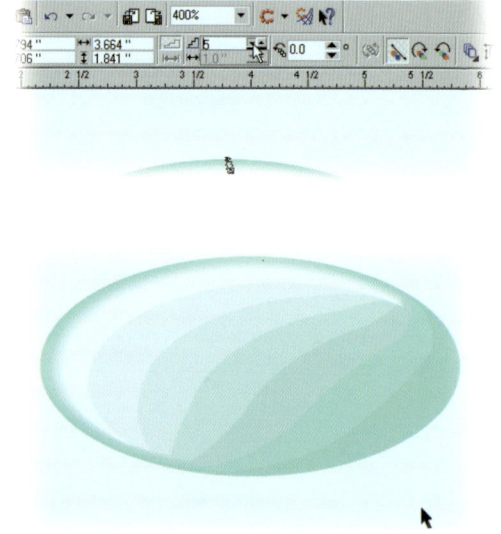

CREATING 3-D EFFECTS · 65

## 3 ADDING A DROP SHADOW

- With the **Pick Tool**, click on the object that you want to apply a drop shadow.
- Here we are going to apply a drop shadow to a spiral created earlier ⬚. The line of the spiral has been thickened to show the shadow more clearly ⬚.

- Select the **Interactive Drop Shadow Tool** from the **Interactive Tool** flyout in the toolbox.

- Go to the property bar and click on the down arrow next to **Presets**. A drop-down menu will appear.

- Choose a shadow from the **Preset** list. Here, we are looking at the shadow named **Pers Bottom Left**.
- The thumbnail display shows how the shadow will lie in relation to the object.

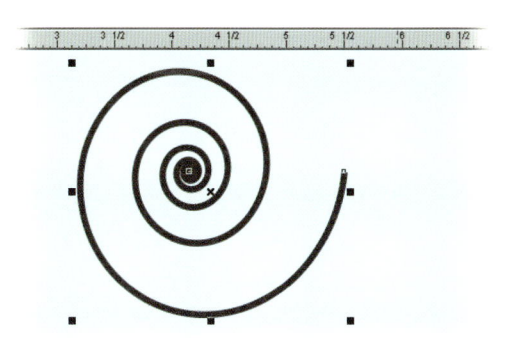

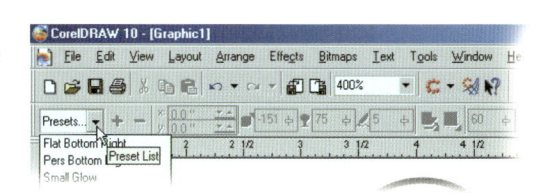

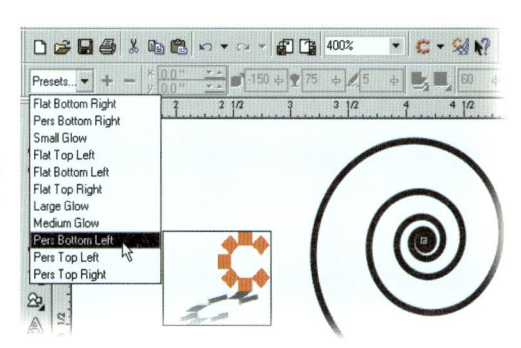

| 33 | Generating Spirals |
| 24 | Adjusting the Line Thickness |

- Clicking on the name of the shadow in the **Preset** list has the effect of applying the shadow to the object.

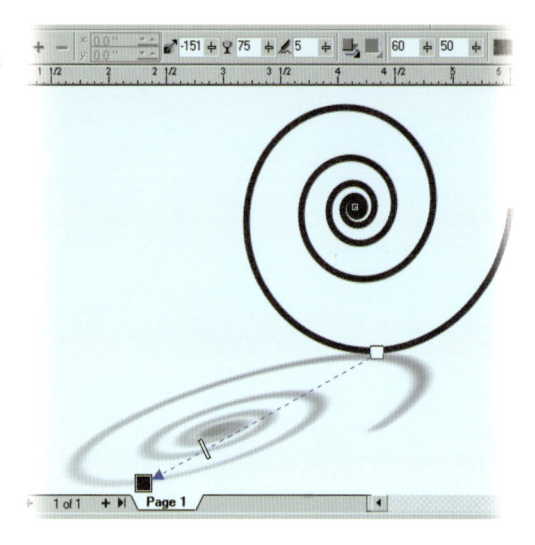

- Color the shadow by selecting a color from the **Drop Shadow Color** drop-down menu.

### DROP SHADOWS

- Drop shadows can be added to objects, groups of objects, artistic text, paragraph text, and bitmapped images.
- Once you have added a drop shadow to an object, you can alter its perspective by clicking on it with the **Interactive Drop Shadow Tool** and dragging the shape.

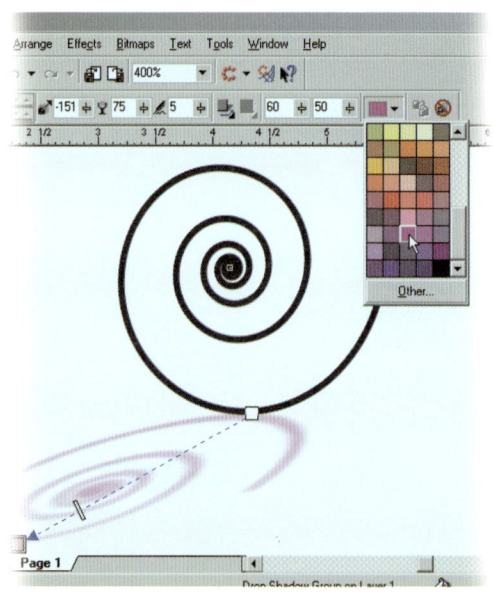

CREATING 3-D EFFECTS · 67

## 4 USING THE EXTRUDE TOOL

● We want to extrude the star shape that we created from the **Preset Star Shapes** in the **Perfect Shapes** flyout.
● First, select the star with the **Pick Tool** from the toolbox.

● Next, select the **Interactive Extrude Tool** from the **Interactive Tool** flyout in the toolbox.

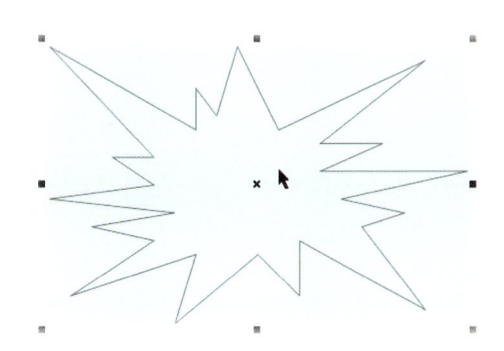

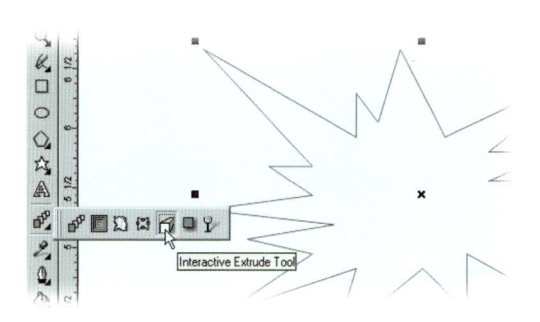

● Click on the object and drag. You will see two joined rectangles. The red rectangle shows the space occupied by the object as it is, and the blue one shows where the extrusion will end.

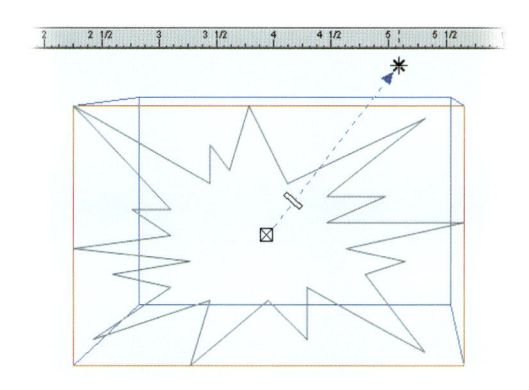

34 **Choosing Predefined Shapes**

## 68 • 3-D EFFECTS

● For a shaded effect, first click on the **Color** icon in the property bar.

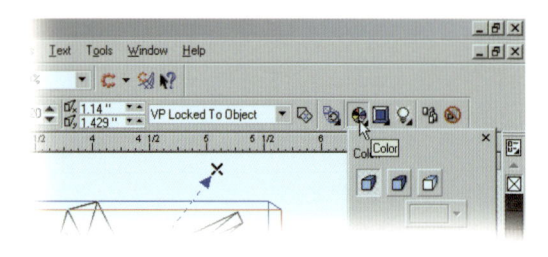

● Select **Use Color Shading** in the **Color** drop-down panel.

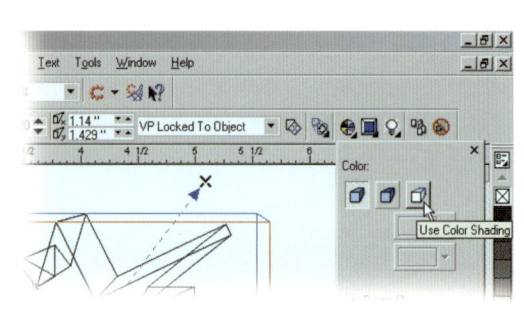

● Choose different colors from the **From** and **To** drop-down menus.

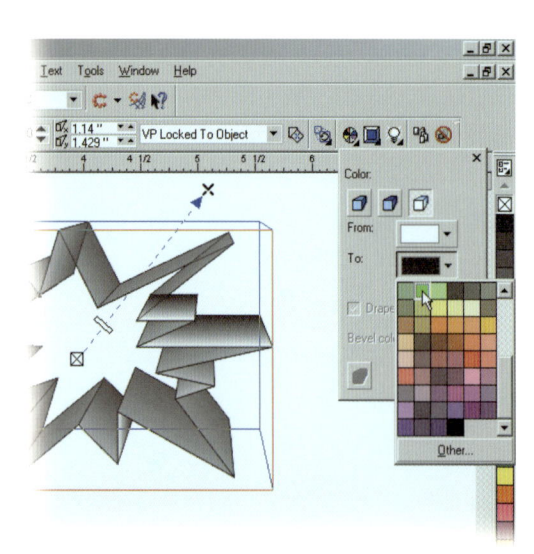

## CREATING 3-D EFFECTS • 69

- Open the **Lighting** options menu from the property bar.

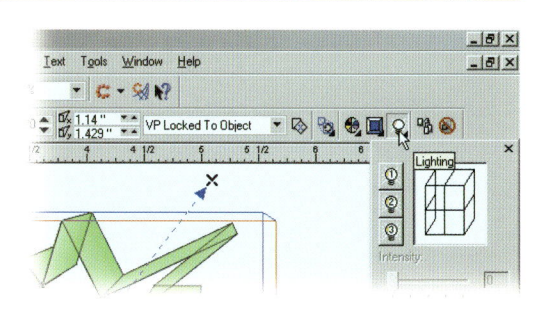

- You can have three light sources. Click on **Light #1** to turn on one light.

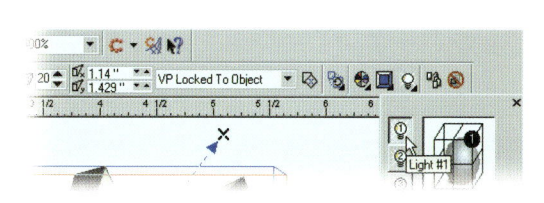

- Click and drag the light to any position on the grid, for different effects.
- Select the **Pick Tool** and click away from the extruded object to see your final results.

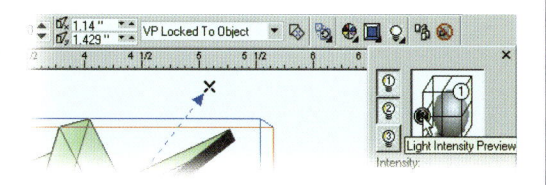

# GLOSSARY

**ARTISTIC TEXT**
A type of text most often used for headings rather than blocks of text. Many special effects can be applied to artistic text such as fitting it to a path, extruding, and enveloping.

**BITMAP**
A particular type of image file that stores the image only in terms of black and white. A bitmapped image is generally used to define line art because its elements can only be black and white.

**CLIPART**
Ready-made images that can be imported into CorelDRAW and edited if required.

**CMYK**
A set of colors made up of varying percentages of cyan (C), magenta (M), yellow (Y), and black (K).

**CURSOR**
An on-screen indicator for the position of the mouse in relation to the monitor. The shape of the cursor changes depending on the tool or command selected.

**DOCKER**
A dialog window containing commands that can remain open or closed until needed.

**DRAWING PAGE**
The portion of the drawing window surrounded by a rectangle and a shadow. Objects not on the drawing page cannot be printed.

**DRAWING WINDOW**
The area around the drawing page. This is a large storage area. Objects placed here will not be printed unless they are moved onto the drawing page.

**DROP SHADOW**
A colored or shaded box or character copy, which is placed behind and/or below an identical box or character to give a shadow effect.

**FILL**
To paint the inside of an enclosed object. You can choose a color and/or a pattern and then paint the object with a fill tool. The area that is painted is called the fill area.

**FLASH**
A light effect to convey the impression of a 3-D effect.

**FLYOUT**
A menu containing related tools, which is opened by clicking and holding the cursor on the visible tool in the toolbox. Flyouts have a black triangle in one corner.

**FOUNTAIN FILL**
Two or more colors blended together in a variety of gradients and applied as a fill.

**GUIDELINE**
Dotted straight lines that can be dragged into position to aid the positioning of objects.

**NODES**
The square shapes at the end of a line segment. Drag one or more of the nodes to alter the shape of a line or a curve.

**OBJECT**
Any element that can be modified. Lines, curves, symbols, shapes, images, and text are all objects.

**PARAGRAPH TEXT**
With paragraph text, you can flow text between text frames, wrap text around objects, and manipulate the size and shape of the text frames.

**PATH**
A path is the basic component that makes up any object. Paths can be open, for example, lines or curves, or they can be closed, for example, a circle or a rectangle. They can consist of a single section or many joined together.

**SELECTION BOX**
An invisible rectangle with eight visible handles that appears around any object selected with the Pick tool.

**SKEWING HANDLES**
Double-headed arrows around the selection box when an object is double-clicked with the Pick tool. Dragging the handles skews the object.

**START NODE**
The large square that appears at the beginning of a line or curve, when the object is selected with the shape tool.

**THUMBNAILS**
Small representations of images in a low resolution.

**UNIFORM FILL**
A single solid color applied as one type of fill.

# INDEX

## AB
3-D effects 62–9
Artistic Media Tool 25–7
artistic text 46–51
Auto-Close Curve button 23
blending 57–9, 63–4
brush styles 25–6

## C
clipart 55
CMYK palette 56
color
   blending 57–9
   CMYK palette 56
   drop shadows 66
   extruded objects 68
   outlines 57
Conical fountain fills 58
CorelTUTOR 12
Curve flyout 10, 22
customizing
   page size 13
   toolbars 11

## D
deleting pages 14–15
dockers 42, 48
documents, multipage 15–17
drawing
   Artistic Media Tool 25–6
   Auto-Close Curve 23
   ellipses 30–1
   freehand 22–3
   lines 22–7
   outlines 22–7
   pie shapes 30–1
   polygons 31–3
   predefined shapes 34–5
   rectangles 28–9
   spirals 33–4
   squares 29
   stars 31–3
drawing window 12
drop shadows 65–6

## E
editing nodes 23–4
ellipses 30–1
envelopes 48–9
extruded objects 67–9

## FG
Fill flyout 10, 57, 60
fills 56–61
fitting text to path 50–1
flowing paragraph text 53
flyout toolbars 10
fonts 46–7, 53
fountain fills 57–9
freehand drawing 22–3
guidelines 17–21

## I
inserting pages 14
Interactive Blend Tool 63
Interactive Drop Shadow Tool 65
Interactive Extrude Tool 67
Interactive Tool flyout 10, 63, 65
intersecting shapes 44–5
irregular shapes 42–3

## LMN
labeled text frames 54
launching CorelDRAW 7
lighting effects 63–4, 69
Linear fountain fills 58
lines 22–7
locking guidelines 21
mirroring effects 36
multipage documents 15–17
nodes 22–4

## O
Object flyout 10, 31, 33
objects
   extruded 67–9
   intersecting 44–5
   mirroring 36
   perspective 62–3
   reflections 63–4
   rotating 38
   selecting 37
   shadow effects 65–6
   shaping 39–45
   skewing 37
   snapping to guidelines 21
   transforming 36–8
   trimming 39–41
   welding 42–3
opening drawing window 12
orientation of page 13
outlines 22–7, 57

## P
page
   deletion 14–15
   insertion 14
   order 17
   orientation 13
   setting up 12–21
   size 13, 15–16
Page Sorter View 15, 16
paragraph text 52–5
path fitting 50–1
Perfect Shape flyout 10, 34–5, 67
perspective 62–3, 66
Pick Tool 37
pie shapes 30–1
polygons 31–3, 44–5
preset envelopes 48
preset guidelines 19–20
preset page sizes 13
preset shapes 34–5, 67
property bars 10

## R
Radial fountain fills 58
rectangles 28–9, 44–5
reflection effect 63–4
rotating
   guidelines 18
   objects 38
rounding rectangle corners 29

## S

selecting
  fonts 46–7, 53
  objects 37
  page details 13
shading extruded objects 68
shadow effect 65–6
Shape Edit flyout 23
shapes
  drawing 28–35
  intersecting 44–5
  irregular 42–3
  predefined 34–5
shaping
  objects 39–45
  text 48–9
shaping handles 22
skewing objects 37
snapping to guidelines 21
special fills 57–61
spinning star effect 33
spirals 33–4, 65–6
spraying 26–7
Square fountain fills 58
squares 29
stars
  drawing 31–3
  extruded 67–9
  intersecting shapes 44–5

## T

text
  artistic 46–51
  fitting to path 50–1
  font choice 46–7, 53
  paragraph 52–5
  perspective 62–3
  shadow effect 66
  shaping 48–9
text frames 54
Texture fills 60–1
thickness of lines 24
thumbnails 15, 16
tools 8–11
  Artistic Media 25–7
  Ellipse 30
  Freehand 22
  Interactive Blend 63
  Interactive Drop Shadow 65
  Interactive Extrude 67
  Pick 37
  Polygon 31
  Rectangle 28
  Shape 22, 23–4
  Spiral 33
  Text 46, 52
transforming objects 36–8
trimming objects 39–41

## U–Z

Uniform fills 56–7
user interface 9
welcome screen 12
welding objects 42–3
window, CorelDRAW 8–9
wrapping text 54–5

# ACKNOWLEDGMENTS

PUBLISHER'S ACKNOWLEDGMENTS
Dorling Kindersley would like to thank the following:
Paul Mattock of APM, Brighton, for commissioned photography.

Screen shots of CorelDRAW © Copyright 2000 Corel Corporation
and Corel Corporation Limited, reprinted by permission.

Screen shots of Microsoft® Windows used
by permission from Microsoft Corporation.

Microsoft® is a registered trademark of Microsoft Corporation.

*Every effort has been made to trace the copyright holders.
The publisher apologizes for any unintentional omissions and would be pleased,
in such cases, to place an acknowledgment in future editions of this book.*

All other images © Dorling Kindersley.
For further information see: www.dkimages.com